MYSELF AS ANOTHER

MYSELF AS ANOTHER

A Journey to the Heart of
Who We Are

John McNerney

NEW CITY PRESS
Enkindling the Spirit of Unity

Published by New City Press
202 Comforter Blvd., Hyde Park, NY 12538
www.newcitypress.com
©2024 John McNerney

Myself as Another: A Journey to the Heart of Who We Are
John McNerney

Cover art:
Jack B. Yeats, "Men of Destiny," 1946.
© National Gallery of Art, Ireland
Used with permission.

Layout by Miguel Tejerina, Gary Brandl

Library of Congress Control Number: 2024931720

ISBN: 978-1-56548-595-2 (paper)
ISBN: 978-1-56548-596-9 (e-book)

Printed in the United States of America

Contents

Acknowledgments 7

Foreword 9

One
Introduction: The Search for *Who* I Am 15

Two
Daniel O'Connell (1775–1847) and Frederick Douglass (1818–1895):
    A Narrative on "Fraternity" 33

Three
St. John Henry Newman (1801–1890):
    "Heart to Heart" in Education 42

Four
Søren Kierkegaard (1813–1855): Stages on Life's Way 48

Five
Ludwig Wittgenstein (1809–1951): A Personal Odyssey 56

Six
Gabriel Marcel (1889–1973): A Philosopher of "Presence" 63

Seven
Edith Stein (1891–1942): Stairway to the "Other" 71

Eight
Viktor Frankl (1905–1997): A Why to Live For 79

Nine
Hannah Arendt (1906–1975): New Beginnings 87

Ten
Dietrich Bonhoeffer (1906–1945):
    Journey to the Center of the Person 93

Eleven
Alfred Delp, SJ (1907–1945): Epiphany of the Person 100

Twelve
Emmanuel Levinas (1901–1995): A Spirituality of "Proximity" 106

Thirteen
Simone Weil (1909–1943): "Gravity" and "Grace" of *Who* We Are 112

Fourteen
Paul Ricoeur (1913–2005): Oneself as Another 118

Fifteen
Etty Hillesum (1914–1943): The Girl who Learned to Kneel 125

Sixteen
Jacques Derrida (1930–2004): A Politics of Friendship 131

Seventeen
Pope Francis: On the Forgotten Dimension of Fraternity 140

Eighteen
David Walsh: The Priority of the Person 146

Afterword 159

Notes 163

Selected Bibliography 189

Acknowledgments

Profound gratitude to my cherished identical twin-brother, Eamonn. Thanks to Michael, Gerardene, Sara, Louise, and Michael Jr. To Brendan, David, Gail, Hugh, Suzanne, James, and Eddie without whom this project would not have been realized. I thank all my Washington, DC friends: Sal, Ruadhrí, George, Dan, Charles, J.J., Marie, Sara, Denis, Kenny, Michael, Debbie, Kate, Ronald, Peter, Thomas, Hunter, and Madeleine and Paul. Thanks to my wonderful teaching colleague at The Catholic University of America, Elizabeth, and all who know me there. I also thank the rector, faculty, staff and students, and especially the Basselin Scholars at The Theological College in Washington, DC. Appreciation goes to Tom, Greg, Gary, and the staff at New City Press, New York. I acknowledge my Irish friends too: Sr. Bernadette, Anne, Caroline, Jacqueline, Brona, Laura, Marie, Liam, and so many others. *Go raibh míle maith agaibh.*

Foreword

Reading *Myself as Another* reminded me of Elgar's *Enigma Variations*, fifteen beautiful movements, each dedicated to one of his friends—the first to his wife, Caroline, the last to himself. He dedicated the *Variations* to "my friends pictured within." And you can feel that each of John McNerney's eighteen brief explorations here have become his "friends pictured within." Readers of this book, I think, will find its subjects become our friends too. Befriended by such luminous friends, we could become better friends to ourselves and to others.

Again and again, as I listened to John's "variations," they brought me to the inner life of some of the more knotty people here—a Ludwig Wittgenstein or a Jacques Derrida, for example. By getting to the heart of each one, John made even these complicated persons "others" unrevealed to me in my previous readings of them.

Seven are Jewish, three Protestant, and others Catholic—but each comes across as a brother or sister united by their discovery of their "who" in their reaching out to "you." For many of the twentieth-century "variations," the historical backdrop to their exploration was the totalitarian canceling, the murder of millions of human beings who were mere "its" for the Nazis. Victor Klemperer (1881–1960), a German scholar, describes the gradual narrowing of his world during 1930s Dresden in his diaries, *I Shall Bear Witness* and *To the Bitter End*. As Jewish, he had to leave his job as a professor of Romance languages, then lose his car, his bicycle, his apartment, and even his pet cat, only escaping during the Allied bombing of Dresden in February 1945. But he and his non-Jewish wife's love for each other overcame the lethal hatred of the regime, and his writings continue to bear witness to the indestructibility of who they were.

Elgar never really explained the "enigma"—maybe it was some concealed leitmotiv of his *Variations*. But a few words may be offered as a help to unpacking the underlying common thread of John's "variations." To do that, I will follow the steps of the Ukrainian-born Jewish philosopher, Martin Buber (1878–1965). According to his biographer, Maurice Friedman, "the decisive experience of Martin Buber's life" was what Buber later came to describe as the "mismeeting" between himself and his mother, who abandoned her family when he was four. Speaking on the balcony around his home near Lvov at that time, a little girl of only a few years older said to him, "No, she will never come back." Many years later, Buber wrote, "I suspect that all that I have learned in the course of my life about genuine meeting [encounter] had its first origin in that hour on the balcony."[1]

To lead into what became the focus of his work, let us speak of three ways I can relate to another person. There is the relationship I can have with any crowd of people—on the street, in a shop, fellow-travelers on a plane—where I relate to "them" and "they." There are the various role-relationships I can have, as a student with a teacher, a customer with a shop-assistant, a patient with a doctor: each recognizes the other within more or less clearly marked-out limits.

But if we turn to the central theme of Buber's 1923 study, *I and Thou*, we find how he articulates another kind of relationship, where I am relating to another not as an anonymous one of a crowd, nor in terms of a particular task, but as a person, as who he or she is. It is this kind of relationship that Buber wrote of as an I/Thou relationship. Buber tells us that:

> When *Thou* is spoken, the speaker has no thing for his object. For where there is a thing, there is another thing. Every *It* is bounded by others; *It* exists only

through being bounded by others. But when *Thou* is spoken, there is no thing. *Thou* has no bounds.

Just as the melody is not made up of notes nor the verse of words nor the statue of lines, but they must be tugged and dragged till their unity has been scattered into these many pieces, so with the man to whom I say *Thou*. I can take out from him the colour of his hair, or of his speech, or of his goodness. I must continually do this. But each time I do he ceases to be *Thou*. And just as prayer is not in time but time in prayer, sacrifice not in space but space in sacrifice, and to reverse the relation is to abolish the reality, so with the man to whom I say *Thou*. I do not meet with him [primarily] at some time or place or other.

The primary word *I-Thou* can be spoken only with the whole being.... I become through my relation to the *Thou*; as I become *I*, I say *Thou*. All real living is meeting.[2]

In 1953, the writer Aubrey Hodes met Buber in Jerusalem, and told him of his difficulties with a mentally sick relation. Buber

spoke of my involvement with my relative's illness as one of the crucial human encounters.... Her illness, he said, had a hidden significance for my own life. Only I could discover the meaning it held for me. But in order to do so I had to check my unconscious view of her as a person who was being drained of her human shape and becoming a thing, an object. I had to penetrate through the skin of her sickness to the basic unchanged humanity, enter her world, but with understanding, not with pity, concerning myself directly with her recovery. And, in doing so, I might discover the deeper meaning of my existence and my capacity for love. Otherwise I would not be able to reach her, and would not be able to unlock the riddle of my responsibility towards her.

For I had a responsibility, he said. Love was responsibility for the loved person by the one who loved. Only by accepting this responsibility could I affirm my real self, my authentic personality. The situation called upon me to make a concrete commitment, to realize my responsibility in action—to see her as a single, unique, distressed individual, not just one of a depersonalized throng of mental patients.[3]

So when I refuse to accept any so-called I/They or I/You relation as enough, there is a challenge to widen them out to the scope of the I/Thou relation. I must do all I can to personalize even apparently transient encounters with others; otherwise, I will have failed the core topic of this book, which is that each other is a part of myself and I a part of them. All of John's protagonists overcome the challenge each other poses to them in time and space, and somehow, transcending those limits of time and space, become the other and thus become themselves.

In his chapter on "The Neighbor," in *Person and Act*, Karol Wojtyla enriched the French philosopher Emmanuel Levinas's focus on the "Other," and the cumulative effect of the "variations" here is that John's *Myself as Another* draws us into a shared we-communion.[4] Further, several of the partners in dialogue with us in this study are quite clear that underlying the I/Thou relationship between myself and the Other, is a deeper relationship each of us has, whether aware of it or not, with the eternal Thou. As Edith Stein put it in her *Finite and Eternal Being* (1936), the riddle of the I remains because "I am not by myself (not a being *a se* and *per se*), and by myself I am nothing; at every moment I find myself face to face with nothingness, and from moment to moment I must be endowed and re-endowed with being.

And yet this empty existence that I am is *being*, and at every moment I am in touch with the fulness of being."[5]

So each person is fundamentally a You-for-God, a Thou for the divine I AM. Not only is the Other more than an Other: he or she is my neighbor. And in some way, God too enters into our space-time transcending dialogue as a divine partner in eternity. The more we allow the "variations" contained in *Myself as Another* to interact with our own open quest for relationship, the more the "enigma" behind them all will reveal itself as Love.

Brendan Purcell
University of Notre Dame, Australia

One

Introduction: The Search for *Who* I Am

In today's world, there is no doubting the importance of the question we pose throughout this book, that is, asking *who* we are as human persons. Indeed, the question "who am I?" has multidimensional implications on the individual, spiritual, economic, and political levels.[1] Therefore it is, as St Augustine says, an issue and question "ancient and so new."[2] Plato, in the *Gorgias*, explains to Chaerephon that if he really wants to know what Gorgias's art [skill] is, then ask him "*who he is*" [447d, my emphasis]. In the *Republic*, we also see Plato outline how the *polis* (political reality) is the human being written large. In other words, it is an expression of *who* we are as human beings.

In Mark's Gospel, we similarly see the identity question clearly emerging. As Jesus walks north toward Caesarea Philippi, we hear him ask his disciples, "Who do you say that I am?" (Mk 8:27–30). Consequently, when we ask "Who am I?" it sets off a whole symphony of explorations that equally reverberate and remain unfinished for each one of us. If the truth be told, it is a never-ending story retelling itself anew in our own lives. It is surely true to say that only persons *know* persons. But we can easily "unbecome" who we are, and we see this spelled out in some of the chapters of *Myself as Another*, where the experiences of alienation undergone in the concentration camps are recounted and philosophically reflected upon. These shed light upon the horrendous ideological blackspots in our history that blinded us from the truth of *who* we are.

In the *Confessions*, St Augustine discovers a need to move beyond his own limitations and inadequacies if he is going to come to terms with knowing who he is as a human being. Following the death of his dear friend Nebridius, he describes how "black grief closed my heart." He says, "My eyes sought him everywhere, but he was missing." Augustine observes, "*I had become a great enigma to myself, and I questioned my soul.*" In other words, he "became a question to himself" because of the loss of his friend, an experience that was a huge suffering for him. During this time, Augustine describes his own fear of death, but he comes to the insight that "Woe to the madness which thinks to cherish human beings as though more than human." He confesses, "I should have lifted . . . [my soul] up to you, Lord."[3] In other words, Augustine must "exit" himself in order to understand his own uniqueness as a human being. The question posed in *Myself as Another*, in the last analysis, can only be addressed by "going beyond" ourselves. The issue of *who* I am involves us in the discovery that I can speak of myself in terms of "another" who is "other" than myself.

Undoubtedly, the question of our identity as persons is, as we have said, a "many-layered" reality and actually resists "any easy synthesis."[4] Thomas Aquinas even said, "No philosopher has ever been able to grasp the being of a single fly."[5] Indeed, in "What is it like to be a bat?" the philosopher Thomas Nagel poses a somewhat similar dilemma in terms of other "beings" and their knowability by us. He asks, for example, how can we ever get to "the inner life of the bat from our own case." He is not just concerned with "what would it be like for *me* to behave as a bat behaves." Nagel's question is much deeper; it is to know "What is it like for a *bat* to be a bat."[6] Actually, although he does not explicitly say so, in asking "what is it like to be. . .?" Nagel is already revealing something of our uniqueness as human beings. It is *we* as persons who have this unique capacity to put ourselves in the place of the "other" and ask, "what is it like to be. . .?" We can pose these kinds of questions because we actually "know what it is like to be us."⁷ But there again, in our world, there is even perplexity and debate in admitting that we have this in common. We can often act as if we are islands entirely unto ourselves, which is indeed very far from the poet John Donne's adage that "no man is an island entire of itself; every man is a piece of the continent, a part of the main."⁸ In the face of such challenges to the question of *who* we are, we can easily become paralyzed by the demands of the task. Actually, Meno in Plato's dialogue complains how Socrates is like "the flat sting ray that one meets in the sea. Whenever anyone comes in contact with it, it numbs him." But Socrates says that he is not interested just in confounding other people for the sake of it. "The truth," he says, is that he infects them "with the perplexity" he experiences in himself. He is, in fact, ready to carry out "a joint investigation and inquiry," and this is also the intention of *Myself as Another*.⁹

Doubtless, *who* we are is guarded by profound mystery pervaded often by the presence of absence. And while we might know and recognize each other as persons we can never reach "any definitive or exhaustive understanding" of this reality.¹⁰ Nonetheless, Nagel's example of a person asking, "What is it like to be a bat?" shows how human beings can set themselves aside in trying to understand another being. Because of this, we can say that human beings are, in fact, "beyond being" as such.¹¹ They are essentially "self-transcenders," meaning that they go beyond themselves and consequently create relationships with others. Indeed, the French philosopher Emmanuel Levinas described this reality when he said that the unique characteristic of human beings is how they live the "priority of the other."¹² And so, to do this, you must forget yourself. Forget in order to be *who* you are. Jesus suggests this personalistic perspective when he recommends "Those who lose their life for my sake will find it" (Mt 16:25).

In fact, as we will see clearly outlined in this book, "person means relation."[13] Humans are *"relaters."* As Martin Buber said, "in the beginning is relation."[14] So too, the Scottish personalist philosopher John Macmurray describes how human beings' proper existence is "as a community of persons in relation." In fact, "The personal relations of persons is constitutive of personal existence," which brings us beyond any merely individualistic or cognitional characterization of the experience of personhood.[15] Indeed this points to a person's total "uniqueness, incomparability, and therefore, nonrepeatability," which can easily be occluded and forgotten about within our present culture.[16] Of course, we constantly run the risk of being "impersonal," and then the whole experience of depersonalization emerges. But this happens exactly because we are "persons." We can only give a name to these pulverizing experiences precisely because we are persons.[17]

In fact, the reality of *who* we are as persons "involves [the possibility of] its own negation." We can easily lose the reality of being persons since "only a person can behave impersonally."[18] In this book, we will hear about people whose lives give witness to the fact that I can only live and be "myself" as "another." The "mother and child" reality is a good example of this, of how person fundamentally means relation.[19] Human experience is "shared experience . . . a common life . . . a reference to the personal Other." We exist not as individuals but as "two persons in personal relation . . . in virtue of our relation to one another. The personal is constituted by personal relatedness. The unit of the personal is not the 'I,' but the 'You and I.'"[20] This applies equally to unborn children since they are "the purest possibility of the person. Of that which *is* without visible manifestation."[21] The "other" defines me as a person, and this is not reducible to tangible components. It is not I who define the "other" but they who define me.

I hope that *Myself as Another* is a development on the Delphic oracle's imperative "know thyself," meaning that we cannot do this unless we realize "that our existence depends upon the existence of the O[o]ther."[22] I can know myself only through "another." These short chapters will help us catch a glimpse of our "person-reality," thus unfolding *who* we are. It is all too easy to give in, as Socrates says, to the easy option of skepticism, thinking that since we do not know then we cannot know what we are to look for.[23] This is why in *Myself as Another*, we positively explore and excavate the writings of political leaders, psychiatrists, and philosophers because the subject of personal identity is ever emergent in them, and its reality is disclosed in all of its truth, splendor, and persistent challenges. The search for the meaning of *who* we are is, for example, traced in chapters like the one on the friendship between the Irish political leader Daniel O'Connell and the African-American abolitionist Frederick Douglass. What emerges here is a beautiful narrative on the meaning of "fraternity," showing how O'Connell and Douglas saw each other primarily as "persons," revealing vital, important political implications in these insights. Their story is largely unknown but uncovers how it was through the power of the language of people like the Irishman O'Connell that Douglass discovers the beauty and worth of his own being as a human person.

In the chapter on St John Henry Newman, reflections on *being persons* are given in a discussion of his "heart speaks to heart" perspective in education. His person-centered approach goes beyond purely intellectual concerns. Education is not just the result of syllogistic reasoning, but is effectively about the direct apprehension of reality through the "other." Speaking about the power of personal influence in education, Newman explains how it is "the personal presence of a teacher. . . . It is the living voice, the breathing form, the expressive countenance" that ultimately educates.

In *An Essay in Aid of a Grammar of Ascent*, Newman explains, "The heart is commonly reached, not through the reason... but by the testimony [of others].... Persons influence us, voices melt us, looks subdue us, deeds inflame us." He observes how many a person will "live and die upon a dogma" but nobody will be "a martyr for a conclusion... no one... will die for his own calculations: he dies for realities."[24] Throughout *The Idea of a University*, Newman argues for a "wholeness of view" in terms of education. If we eclipse the person-centric approach to teaching, we can end up trying to understand Hamlet without the Danish Prince. The "truth" of the "person" is not "only a portion, but a condition of general knowledge."[25]

In "Søren Kierkegaard: Stages on Life's Way," we see how Kierkegaard outlined the fundamental challenge in life as concerning not "what am I to know" but *"what am I to do."* He says, "The thing is to find a truth which is true *for me*, to find *the idea for which I can live or die.*"[26] He places the imperative on "living" and actively participating in the stages of life's way. In "Ludwig Wittgenstein: A Personal Odyssey," we discover how our use of language uniquely discloses the nature of being human. At the same time, Wittgenstein was always keenly conscious of the "mystery" of *who* we are; indeed, he famously ends his book *Tractatus Logico-Philosophicus* with the enigmatic words, "Whereof one cannot speak, thereof one must be silent."[27] For Wittgenstein, "Philosophy is not a theory but an activity."[28] For him, the human being is engaged in action and not an abstraction. Wittgenstein reflects that we should not just assume that the meaningful is limited only to what we speak about or can put into words. Meaning in life reveals itself in living and not—as Newman highlights— in logical analysis. It has not just notional but real existential significance. Wittgenstein was fond of saying that nothing can be its own explanation, which is especially evident regarding knowing *who* I am as a human person. Its unfolding necessarily involves the "other" and cannot be explained in terms of a "solitary" understanding of ourselves. We can say that "the Self as Subject is the isolated self" and is not *who* I am. Myself "exists only in dynamic relation with the Other."[29] Descartes's motto was "I think, therefore I am," but we can assert instead, "Myself as Another, therefore I am." Wittgenstein is normally known as a philosopher of language. In his early writings, he describes how "language disguises" thought with clothes that do not allow "the form of the body to be recognized."[30] In my view, and I outline this in *Myself as Another*, behind his reflections on language, *we* can find an emergent "person-centric" perspective. Words may have the meaning we give them, yet it is persons using the words that constitutes their meaning.[31]

This emerges, of course, not by means of any simple analysis based on solipsistic abstraction but very clearly by reflecting on the lived experiences of those who were both victims and survivors of the Holocaust. We focus on these in *Myself as Another*. Such cathartic events are seen through the firsthand stories of Edith Stein, Etty Hillesum, Dietrich Bonhoeffer, Alfred Delp, SJ, and Viktor Frankl. Stein helps us to ascend the stairway to the "other," helps us understand that not all problems can be solved, but they can be loved. This is clearly evidenced in her way of life, which was a going beyond herself in living out "empathy" for each one she encountered. She lived out the reality "person means relation." The chapter "Etty Hillesum: The Girl Who Learned to Kneel" makes it clear that the time for armchair theorizing is over. Through her suffering, she learns of the need for an inner sculpting that gives rebirth to *who* she is as a person. In the chapter "Dietrich Bonhoeffer: Journey to the Center of the Person," we read in his *Letters and Papers from Prison* the words: "Who am I? They mock me, they mock me, these lonely questions of mine. Whoever, I am, You know, O God,

I am Yours."³² We discover that the unravelling of human identity lies in a movement that transcends the limits of my own self and that which the world imposes upon me. Human freedom can be lived even when I am exteriorly unfree. Bonhoeffer was an embattled witness to this very truth. In a very moving letter to his friends written before his execution at Flossenbürg concentration camp, he speaks about the pain of separation and how the ultimate one of death does not negate *who* we are as human persons. Yes, he says, the departure of loved ones causes us great pain and separation, but we somehow remain connected to the other person "through the emptiness" we experience. God does not fill the vacuum and it is nonsense to say so; "Rather [He] keeps it empty and thus helps preserve . . . our authentic communion."³³ In fact, Bonhoeffer says, we search for stronger bonds of communion with the departed person. He testifies to the reality that the human person is beyond "being" as such.

The modern Greek philosopher Christos Yannaras's observations are insightful here. He says that "Being-here" ('*Da-sein*'), which defines the *reality* of human existence, refers not to a dimensional hereness, but to the immediacy of *ecstatic* relation. The existential reality of personal (ecstatic) relation does not acknowledge any restrictions of place.³⁴ Yannaras speaks of "*personal relation as existential ek-stasis*," that is, a "going beyond" which is "identified with the actualization of the person's otherness."³⁵ In the chapter reflecting on the German Jesuit Alfred Delp, we discover how his life was a continual Advent, that is, an epiphany and living out the truth of who we are. In a novel deconstruction of the language of "self-fulfillment," he outlines how "unless a person reaches out. . . the only alternative is to vegetate." In fact, if we just stagnate then we end up "by becoming less human."³⁶

The reflections by Viktor Frankl, the Austrian psychiatrist and philosopher who survived the concentration camps, confirm even more these intuitions into *who* we are as persons. Truly, the analyses Frankl carried out in the Nazi death camps unearth the hidden roots of the human person that no ideology can annihilate, and we take a look at these in the section devoted to him in *Myself as Another*. Frankl's parents, brother, and pregnant wife all perished in the camps. His investigations, which are not just diagnostic but therapeutic, reveal how those who survived the atrocious circumstances were those who had existential meaning. Adapting Friedrich Nietzsche's motto, Frankl notes that "he who has a *why* to live for could bear with almost any *how*."[37] In other words, people who *lived* the *why* without the answer could somehow hold on to some type of personal dignity. It was, in fact, by letting go and not clinging to reinforced notions of their own self-enclosed identities that they realized and lived *who* they were as human beings. In these experiences of profound suffering, they *became* who they are as persons. Frankl comments on how he and others "had to teach the despairing men that *it did not really matter what we expected from life, but rather what life expected from us.*" When we come to question the meaning of life, we cannot answer with sweeping generalizations. "Life," says Frankl, "does not mean something vague, but something real and concrete." Even in suffering, the uniqueness of human beings shines forth; a unique horizon opens and the "opportunity lies in the way in which he [the human person] bears" the burden.[38]

"Hannah Arendt: New Beginnings" discusses the German-born American political philosopher's insightful writings on the nature of human action. Arendt outlines how in action the "identity" of *who* we are is uniquely disclosed. She unearths the ever important need to tell the story of human action, since through a community of memory it preserves our reality as human beings. Indeed, Arendt's theory on human agency makes an original contribution to twentieth-century political thought. We can see traces of this unique analysis and approach in her famous study *Eichmann in Jerusalem,* on the trial of the Nazi leader, which originally appeared as a series of articles in *The New Yorker*.[39] Eichmann lost touch with the reality that person means "relation." Arendt notes, "Eichmann's opportunities for feeling like Pontius Pilate were many, and as the months went by, he lost the need to feel anything at all."[40] In *The Human Condition,* she points out how what she proposes in her investigation is really very simple. It is, she says, "*nothing more than to think what we are doing*" when we act as human persons. [41] Arendt proposes a reconsideration "of the human condition from the vantage point of our newest experiences and our most recent fears."[42] She speaks of how our world is plagued by a kind of thoughtlessness when it comes to understanding ourselves. Focusing on a thoroughgoing inquiry into action reveals the "unique personal identities" of human beings.[43] Arendt writes, "This disclosure of 'who' in contradistinction to 'what' . . . is implicit in everything somebody says or does."[44]

"Emmanuel Levinas: A Spirituality of 'Proximity'" presents the Jewish French philosopher's thoughts on the human person. In *Alterity and Transcendence,* Levinas points out how the reality of the "other" "demands me, requires me, summons me."[45] He explains, "The face-to-face is a relation in which the *I* frees itself from being limited to itself." In the encounter with the other person, we experience an "exodus from that limitation of the *I* to itself."[46] Levinas's emphasis on the "other" points toward understanding transcendence as being "alive in relation to the other man, i.e. in the proximity of one's fellow man, whose *uniqueness* and consequently whose irreducible *alterity*" remains hidden unless we see him face-to-face.[47] Indeed, his perspectives on the significance of the other almost convey the idea of "the sacrament of coexistence."[48] In the encounter with the human, you have the "possible advent of an ontological absurdity."⁴⁹ Levinas says that in such an encounter "the concern for the other is greater than the concern for oneself." This is what he calls "saintliness."

The chapter on the French philosopher Simone Weil unfolds an understanding into how I come to know *who* I am as a human being by "detaching" from myself. She believed that any exit strategy from oppression and alienation as she experienced it under Nazism and then working in labor intensive factories in France cannot be based upon revolutionary or utopic solutions. The Marxian analysis holds, she says, that once you change the external economic and social structures, you totally eradicate alienation. But such transformations are sustainable only if they occur within.⁵⁰ She considers philosophy not to be about the transfer or acquisition of different forms of knowledge. Rather, she says, it is about the "transformation of the orientation of the soul, which we call *detachment*."⁵¹ Real change happens within, and this begins in detachment. In *Gravity and Grace*, she reminds us that "'He emptied himself of his divinity.' To empty ourselves of the world. To take the form of a slave. To reduce ourselves to the point we occupy in space and time— that is to say, nothing. To strip ourselves of the imaginary royalty of the world. . . . Then we possess the truth of the world" and of *who* we are as persons.⁵²

This, of course, requires conversion, which Weil also reflects on in her works. In Plato's texts, she discovers a rich storehouse which she compares to the parables of the Gospels. She draws out from Plato how "what one person can do for another is not to add something to him, but to turn him towards the light that comes from elsewhere, from on high."⁵³ In light of this, *Myself as Another* is not just this book's title, but it is a way of life and conversion. Weil discusses how the least attachment can snare our transformation as persons. She notes, "*A coming short by a single degree of heat can keep wood from being lit . . . as a thread ever so slight can keep a bird from flying, unless it is cut. . . . That is what Plato means by this little phrase: all the soul.*"[54]

In talking about "conversion"—or what Bernard Lonergan calls "a transformation of the subject and his world"—we might think this is a tall order when it comes to human beings. Is it conceivable that a person's eyes can be opened, changing course and direction?[55] We may very well ask: is this achievable? In the chapter "Paul Ricoeur: Oneself as Another," we unearth how human persons have unique capacities, which we all too easily obscure if we forget that the "performative" dimension of human existence is not what constitutes our being as persons. In today's world, we can be quickly reduced to a function, resulting in the experience of alienation that Karl Marx insightfully spoke about. Ricoeur's overall project is to uncover what he calls "the *capable human being* [which often lies hidden] behind the *ineffective human being*, behind the *powerless human being.*" He emphasizes, "It is in the capacity to be Human that the character of being deserving of respect lies."[56]

Indeed, in his work *Oneself as Another*, Ricoeur recovers for us how the "other" is necessarily constitutive of *who* I am. He notes how human action is fundamentally realized "with and for Others," leading to an understanding of human identity. Ricoeur stresses how it is important to live in the reality of giving and receiving even when we can no longer do anything, as when we are ill. In such a scenario, appearance is not reality. Relying on Aristotle's analysis of human friendship, Ricoeur declares that "the friend, inasmuch as he is that other self, has the role of providing what one is incapable of procuring by oneself."[57] It is precisely, in fact, in the human person that we can find "the newness of what is new."[58] In terms of the fragility of our human nature, we can all too easily drown in the pond of disappointment. Ricoeur instead seeks to unlock for us amazement at the human person's capacities. Adapting the words of St. Catherine of Siena, we can say "If we are *who* we should be, we will set the world aflame."[59]

In "Jacques Derrida: The Politics of Friendship," we reflect on the possibility of a politics of friendship which is the consequence of understanding "myself" in terms of the reality of the "other."[60] Such an approach may seem anathema in the prevailing circumstances of social and political polarization.[61] Politics, nonetheless, is essentially about persons, and without them it simply does not exist. Using Derrida's philosophical perspectives in a book devoted to the theme *Myself as Another* may seem somewhat surprising. He is, of course, widely known for the term "deconstruction," probably one of his most controversial ideas. But Derrida said it was a word "whose fortunes have disagreeably surprised me." For Derrida, the meaning of reality is often found in the margins.[62] In his later writings, he proceeds to reflect on friendship because he believes it "has been an apparently marginal concept within the field of politics and of political philosophy for centuries."[63] As Derrida considers the matter, he observes how he has never stopped asking himself "what is meant when one says 'brother,' when someone is called 'brother.'" He asks, "What is the political impact and range of this chosen word?"[64] Derrida, of course, is not alone in considering such themes. In *The Meaning of Christian Brotherhood*, Joseph Cardinal Ratzinger (Pope Benedict XVI) explores the distinctive Christian breakthrough into understanding the meaning of fraternity.[65] Ratzinger traces how Christianity attempts to avoid the "desire to form some self-sufficient esoteric group." While there may be those who are not believers, Christianity fulfills its service "for the others who are, at bottom, the 'other brother' and whose fate is in the hands of the first brother."[66]

In this regard, it is interesting to note in *Democracy in America* how Alexis Tocqueville keenly observed this characteristic of "fraternity." In speaking about the art of politics in the United States, he noted how "Americans of all ages, all conditions, all minds constantly unite" forming associations to work for the good of all. He says he "admired the infinite art with which the inhabitants of the United States managed to fix a common goal to the efforts of many men and to get them to advance to it freely."[67] Indeed, Aristotle considered friendship, which involves "joint perception" or "like-mindedness," as the highest form of politics [*Nicomachean Ethics*, 1170b10–12]. Derrida critically and profitably asks "What would then be the politics" that goes outside the closed boundaries of purely "*familial*" and "*fraternalist*" notions that we might have? What would such a new politics look like? Democracy, Derrida says, "is a promise . . . a promise which will remain a promise" unless we address several urgent problems. He speaks of the challenges of displaced persons, arguing that we must think of "a democratic relationship beyond the borders of the nation-state." All of this requires a "transformation of the concept of the political, of the concept of democracy, and of the concept of friendship."[68]

Given the various reflections offered in *Myself as Another*, the reader might quite rightly comment on how the presentations are rich and engaging but quite simply utopic. Present-day society is very much characterized by disorder and all its discontents.[69] But as human beings, it is we who can ask, "What if?" Toward the end of the book, we turn to the writings of Pope Francis, where we discover insightful thoughts recalling us back to the forgotten dimension of fraternity and its role in society and politics of today.[70] In *Let us Dream*, for example, he describes how "a people can become oblivious to its own history." And there is always the risk "that the people might dissolve into a mere mass, with no unifying principle to bind them." Francis points to the fact that it is often a crisis that allows "a people to recover its memory, and therefore its capacity for action" as human persons.[71] He says the time has come "to restore an ethics of fraternity and solidarity, regenerating the bonds of trust and belonging. For *what saves us is not an idea but an encounter.*" The pope reminds us: "*Only the face of another is capable of awakening the best of ourselves.*"[72]

In the encyclical *Fratelli Tutti*, Francis asks for an important reexamination of our understanding of friendship and the need for nations to build upon the reality of a common fraternity. He describes how "narrow forms of nationalism are an extreme expression of an inability to grasp the meaning" of the need to have a heart open to the whole world. The real worth of a country, he argues, is measured by its "ability to think not simply as a country but also as part of the larger human family."[73] Indeed, it is interesting to note how the Chinese intellectual and political dissident Liu Xiaobo likewise pointed out, "Chinese human beings are no different from human beings anywhere—they want freedom, equality, human rights, and to live in autonomy and dignity." But this "harmonious society can only come into being *when there is trust among the people.*"[74] Love, Xiaobo believed, can be used to dissipate hate. What the Chinese régime fears most, he says, is love because "love produces strength by binding people together."[75]

This is, in fact, what Václav Havel, the former Czech president and dissident, calls the essential "power of the powerless."[76] Havel states in the same essay that the issue "is the rehabilitation of values like trust, openness, responsibility, solidarity, love."[77] Speaking about the Golden Rule, the spiritual founder and writer Chiara Lubich emphasizes how if it is taken seriously, it "would be the greatest inducement to harmony among all kinds of people." She asks us to imagine what "would the world be if not only individuals but whole races and nationalities practiced the 'Golden Rule' in this form: 'Love the other's country as you love your own.'"[78] Indeed, these questions and challenges are not so distant from the insights harvested from the various philosophers and writers we discuss in *Myself as Another*.

In his writings, Pope Francis clearly encourages us to make what I call a discovery of *Myself as Another*. He elaborates for us the importance of becoming *who* we really are as human persons. From his perspective, this is something we cannot easily opt out of. He outlines plainly how the economic or political order we as Christians build or contribute to truly matters. It is, he says, not an optional calling or just an inconvenient truth to be hidden away from us or others. In this context, he suggests, our intelligence, judgment, and creativity unfold. Pope Francis writes how it is in this way that "the beauty [of the] different faces of the one humanity that God so loves" can be realized. In *Fratelli Tutti*, he explains how "love of the other" begins with me and this obviously has consequences in how we put fraternity into practice in the public sphere. There is no room for abstract moralizing or remaining indifferent bystanders because we must begin "case by case, [and] act at the most concrete and local level."[79]

Myself as Another: A Journey to the Heart of Who We Are is not the outlining of another theory about a theory on the human person. It is not an exploration made on intellectual stilts which are "dinosauric," therefore, turning out as very nice academic considerations but being, nonetheless, out of time and place. On the contrary, in these chapters I hope that the reader discovers how, as Emmanuel Levinas says, it is in living out the priority of the other that we become *who* we are as human beings. As we read through this book, it is important to keep in mind that the truth of *who* we are is not just faith-specific. We must remain open to the existential questions. The issue of *who* we are is ultimately guarded by mystery, but we should not then just lock ourselves out of inquiring about this reality. It is surely unadvisable to take the approach of *"denke nicht, frage mich nicht,"* that is, "don't think, don't ask me," because it is too difficult and controversial.[80] Everyone is a candidate for the splendor and beauty of this truth. We are all part of the narrative that recaptures *who* we are, and so we cannot just remain idle spectators. We have a responsibility to tell this story too. To speak about our own odyssey! I hope that some of the experiences described in these chapters find an echo in your own lives and subsequent reflections. Socrates declared that he could "let no day pass without discussing and examining both myself and others." He says it "is really the very best thing" that a person can do and that "life without this sort of examination is not worth living."[81]

In "David Walsh: The Priority of the Person," we introduce the reflections of someone I consider to be one of the most important philosophers on the human person in the English-speaking world. His study, *Politics of the Person*, for example, reveals an insight: "The pathway to understanding reality and ourselves passes not through careful consideration of 'being' and 'existence' but through people" and their encounter with each other.[82] Through the "I" and the "You" of each other as human beings we can comprehend the "Other." From this perspective, politics is not just transactional. It is much more. The realm of the political is the decisive space in which we unfold *who* we are. It is "the vehicle by which the truth of existence is gained or lost for humanity as a whole." The challenge, Walsh suggests, is "that our language, with all of its presumptive metaphysical capacity, has utterly failed to capture this." He outlines how in the political realm we can tease out and reason how "to resist the dominance of the quantifiable" whereby persons are treated just as entities. He argues, "The existence of the polity is secured only by members who are prepared to sacrifice themselves for it." In other words, its life is dependent on living out the priority of the other. This is at the heart of the theme in *Myself as Another*. The signing of a social or political contract will not secure this because a community of persons is made up of those "who have fully transcended themselves."[83] It is a reality whose meaning goes beyond any written text. Indeed, we catch a glimpse of this in our earlier discussion on Daniel O'Connell and Frederic Douglas and their narrative on fraternity. Actually, in the Walshian perspective we begin to discover the virtue of politics, seeing it as a reality in which we can publicly recapture and realize the forgotten dimensions and truth of *who* we are as human persons. W. B. Yeats notes that daily life need not be just about fumbling in the greasy till and adding the halfpence to the pence.[84] As persons, we are an epiphany opening horizons onto the other and to *who* we are. And so, Walsh describes, "The person who can give the response of yes [to the 'other'] is the epiphany of what a person is."[85] It is in relationality that human beings disclose *who* they are. The *how* of this is lived by actions of self-giving and this pertains to those who have gone before us and remains a responsibility to those still alive.[86] And so I hope this small book helps unfold the wealth of *who* we are as human beings and makes it worth living.

Two

Daniel O'Connell (1775–1847) and Frederick Douglass (1818–1895): A Narrative on "Fraternity"

Frederick Douglas Arrives in Ireland

A witness to the beginnings of the horrors of the Irish famine (called *An Gorta Mór, The Great Hunger*) was the African-American abolitionist, Frederick Douglas.[1] He arrived in Ireland in 1845 at the invitation of the Hibernian Anti-Slavery Society, the leading such group in Europe at the time. He traveled to Ireland also for another reason—to put it simply, he was a "wanted man" in his own country. *Narrative of the Life of Frederick Douglass, An American Slave* had just been published in America.[2] He was a fugitive, and his "owners" wanted his capture. Such was the popularity of Douglass's book that a new version, called the second Irish (Dublin) edition (1846), was published while he was visiting Britain and Ireland. In the new preface, Douglass said he felt totally free to state the names of his oppressors.[3] He believed that his book would help "thousands and tens of thousands" of people cooperate in the "overthrow of the meanest, hugest, and most dastardly system of inequity that ever disgraced any country."[4]

Encounter with the "Liberator": Daniel O'Connell

The highlight of his visit to Ireland must have been meeting and hearing the Liberator, the renowned Daniel O'Connell.[5] In 1829, O'Connell achieved Catholic Emancipation, which for the first time gave Catholics the right to vote, to sit in parliament, and to participate freely in public life. So Douglass's and O'Connell's lives intersected, unfurling a new narrative on fraternity for the peoples of America and Ireland. Douglass explains in his *Narrative* how at the age of twelve, he got hold of a book called *The Colombian Orator*. This was a collection of political essays, poems, and dialogues edited and collected by Caleb Bingham. It was published in 1797 and was used by students in American schools. Douglass explains how in this book, he came across speeches about Catholic Emancipation. He mentions in particular a speech by the Irish playwright and political leader Richard Brinsley Sheridan. These and other speeches, he says, were "choice documents to me. I read them over and over again with unabated interest." He describes how they "gave tongue to interesting thoughts of my own soul." Reading these texts gave him a view of his "wretched condition, without the remedy, opening his eyes to the horrible pit he was in." But he still as of yet found "no ladder to get out." Nonetheless, after taking in these breathtaking new insights into *who* we are as human beings, Douglass says,

> The silver trump of freedom had aroused my soul to eternal wakefulness. Freedom now appeared to disappear no more forever. It was heard in every sound and seen in every thing. It was ever present to torment me with a sense of my wretched condition. I saw nothing without seeing it, I heard nothing without hearing it, and felt nothing without feeling it. It looked from every star, it smiled in every calm, breathed in every wind, and moved in every storm.[6]

Discovery of "Personal" Worth

Frederick Douglass discovered in the power of the language of people like Daniel O'Connell the beauty and worth of his own being.[7] This was different from the "valuation" he encountered in the plantations and slave markets. In chapter eight of his *Narrative*, Douglass gives a description of how he is treated as a thing and not a person. His old slave master dies, and the property is divided between the family in order to share the estate. Douglass says, "I was immediately sent for, to be valued with the other property." His anger grows as he now has a new conception of his "degraded condition." He describes, "We were all ranked together at the valuation. Men and women, old and young, married and single were ranked with horses, sheep and swine. *These were horses and men, cattle and women, pigs and children all holding the same rank in the scale of being*, and all were subjected to the same narrow examination."[8]

In the encyclical *Fratelli Tutti*, Pope Francis uses perceptive words on the reality of slavery, which persists in different ways even in our times. He observes how slavery today, as in the past, is "rooted in a notion of the human person that allows him or her to be treated as an object. . . . Whether by coercion, or deception, or by physical or psychological duress, human persons created in the image and likeness of God are deprived of their freedom, sold and reduced to being the property of others. They are treated as means to an end."[9]

"A Tale of Woe"

On his arrival in Ireland, Douglass explained how he saw the "painful exhibitions of human misery, which meet the eye of a stranger almost every step" of the way. When he was in Dublin, he also visited cabins or huts near the city. He was completely shocked by what he saw and experienced. In a letter to the American abolitionist, journalist, and social reformer William Lloyd Garrison, he described how the streets in Dublin were alive with beggars. He says, "Some of them were mere stumps of men, without feet, without legs ... casting sad looks to the right and left, in the hope of catching the eye of a passing stranger."[10] He said:

> Of all places to witness human misery, ignorance, degradation, filth and wretchedness, an Irish hut is pre-eminent.... Here you have an Irish hut or cabin, such as millions of the people of Ireland live in.... Men and women, married and single, lie down together, in much the same degradation as the American slaves.[11]

Douglass easily identified with the Irish. He commented that whoever thinks themselves abolitionist and "yet cannot enter into the wrongs of others, has yet to find a true foundation for his anti-slavery faith. The responsibility to end slavery belonged to Americans as well as the Irish, *but because they [were] MEN.*" He felt all the Irish lacked was "black skin and wooly hair, to complete their likeness to the plantation negro." Douglas pointed out that "slavery was not what took away one right or property in man: it took man himself."[12]

The Liberator's "Sympathy" Unlimited

Frederick Douglass was deeply impressed by Daniel O'Connell when he heard him speak in Conciliation Hall, in Dublin. He said, "His eloquence came down upon the vast assembly like a summer thunder-storm upon a dusty road." The Liberator, by then beset by old age and poor health, devoted a large part of his speech to "the plague spot of slavery" in America. He introduced the young twenty-seven-year-old Douglass to the crowd as "the black O'Connell of the United States," noting that "My sympathy is not confined to the narrow limits of my own green Ireland.... My heart walks abroad.... Wherever the miserable is to be succored, and the slave is to be set free, there my spirit is at home, and I delight to abide in its abode."[13] These words suggest how O'Connell saw the "other" as a "person," which Douglass clearly identified with. Douglass notes that O'Connell was called "The Liberator" and not without cause because he was the friend of the liberty of the human person the world over.[14] When O'Connell died, Douglass felt that "a great champion of freedom had fallen." Douglass harshly criticized O'Connell's successors— "the Duffy's, Mitchells, Meagher's, and others." People, he says, "who loved liberty for themselves and their country, but were utterly destitute of sympathy with the cause of liberty in countries other than their own." [15]

Douglass tells an interesting story about O'Connell's meeting with an American in Ireland. The gentleman offered his hand in greeting, but the Liberator drew back, asking if the American was a slave owner. The man replied: "No . . . I am not . . . but I am willing to discuss the question of slavery with you." O'Connell replied: "Discuss it with me! Without meaning you the least harm in the world, should a gentleman come into my study and propose to discuss with me the rightfulness of picking pockets, I would show him the door, lest he should be tempted to put his theory into practice."[16] O'Connell never forgot to communicate the human face and suffering of slavery. His descriptions moved his audiences to tears. Even Charles Dickens, at the time a parliamentary reporter at the British House of Commons, was moved to tears by his speeches. On one occasion, O'Connell described the slave mother who "looks upon the child she has borne, and knows that she is but rearing the slave of another. . . . Instead of a blessing, she feels that in each child she has been visited with a curse."[17] He invariably saw all issues of injustice through the eyes of the "other."

Riot aboard the *Cumbria*

In his letters and speeches, Douglass continually refers to how throughout life his associations with the Irish acted as a crucial component in his own liberation. On his voyage to Britain and Ireland aboard the Cunard Liner *Cumbria*, he "could not be received onboard as a cabin passenger," so he had to travel in steerage. But he tells that with most passengers, "All color distinctions were flung to the winds, and I found myself treated with every mark of respect, from the beginning to the end of the voyage, except in a single instance."[18] When Douglass was invited to give the passengers a lecture on slavery, those from New Orleans and Georgia took offense and threatened to throw him overboard. But Captain Judkins intervened, along with other passengers, threatening to put the "salt water mobocrats in irons." At that they scampered away "and for the rest of the voyage conducted themselves very decorously."[19] On reaching Liverpool, the pro-slavery Americans went to the press "to justify their conduct" and denounce Douglass "as a worthless and insolent negro." But their protestations backfired, simply securing Douglass a greater audience.

"The Chattel Becomes a Man"

In a letter, one of a series addressed to William Lloyd Garrison, Douglass speaks directly of his homeland and about Ireland: "The land of my birth welcomes me to her shores only as a slave, and spurns with contempt the idea of treating me differently; so that I am an outcast from the society of my childhood, and an outlaw in the land of my birth."[20]

"In Ireland," however, "I was not treated as a color, but as a man—not as a thing, but as a child of the common Father of us all." Traveling from the Hill of Howth to the Giant's Causeway and to Cape Clear in the West, an area covering the whole island from east to west and north to south, Douglass wrote, "I can truly say, I have spent some of the happiest moments of my life since landing in this country. I seem to have undergone a transformation. I live a new life.... Instead of the bright blue sky of America, I am covered with the soft grey fog of the Emerald Isle. I breathe, and lo! The chattel becomes a man."[21]

The "new life" which Douglass speaks about and experiences is that of "fraternity." And this essentially entails seeing the other with "new eyes." He says he gazes around in vain "for one who will question my equal humanity, claim me as a slave.... I find nothing here to remind me of my complexion."[22] "Fraternity" is not an abstract definition to him but is about becoming *who* we are as human persons. It is an existential reality and therefore tangible. Douglass describes the elements of this reality as "glorious enthusiasm," "deep sympathy," "cordiality," "kind hospitality," and a "spirit of freedom."[23]

Acceptance According to *Who* I Am

Douglass was only a few days in Dublin when "a gentleman of great respectability" offered to show him around "through all the public buildings of that beautiful city."[24] He even found himself dining with the Lord Mayor of Dublin. Douglass explains how the people he met "measure and esteem ... [people] according to their moral and intellectual worth, and not according to the color of their skin."[25]

He visited not only Ireland but also England, Scotland, and Wales; it is, he says, to "these friends I owe my freedom."[26] He pointed out that neither in his speech nor his writings did he ever allow himself to simply oppose Americans. He took his stand "on the high ground of human brotherhood.... Slavery is a crime ... against God, and all members of the human family; and it belongs to the whole human family to seek its suppression."[27]

A "Pact of Mercy"

While in England, Douglass wrote a letter, "To My Old Master, Thomas Auld," one of his former slave owners. He does not hold back his condemnation of the evil crimes committed against him by Auld when Douglass was a slave. But in this letter we gain insight into how Douglass saw the "other," in this case his former "owner," with "new eyes" and mercy. He signs the letter, "I am your fellow-man, but not your slave."[28] His letter sums up his life as a mystery in which Douglass seeks to know "Why am I a slave?" He explains how the mystery slowly unfolds, as he discovers *"I am myself; you are yourself; we are two distinct persons, equal persons. What you are I am. You are a man and so am I. God created both."*[29] In conclusion, he writes, "I entertain no malice towards you personally. There is no roof under which you would be more safe than mine.... I should esteem it a privilege to set you an example as to how mankind ought to treat each other." [30] To another of the slave owning family, Hugh Auld, Douglass shows amazing forgiveness, writing: "I feel nothing but kindness for you all—I love you, but hate Slavery."[31] His is a "person-centric" perspective, distinguishing the crime of injustice from the person.

A "Narrative" for Our Times

The O'Connell-Douglass narrative on fraternity is a timely message for America, Ireland, and the world at large. It entails enlarging the human heart to the measure and reality of *who* the other is. We cannot just sit back, for example, asking *"What have we to do with slavery?"*[32] As the Russian writer Aleksandr Solzhenitsyn said, the line dividing good and evil cuts through the heart of every human being. He explains that "this line shifts. Inside us, it oscillates with the years." It is impossible to expel evil and injustice from our world simply by excluding those whose "hearts [are] overwhelmed by evil." During the lifetime of each person, this dividing line keeps changing places even within us. But we can constrict such iniquities by treating the other as myself.[33] So it is up to us to write and give an account of *who* we truly are as human beings. This will be a precious narrative for our times.

Three

St. John Henry Newman (1801–1890): "Heart to Heart" in Education

The Idea of a University

It is interesting that one of the first students to frequent John Henry Newman's newly founded university (1854) in Dublin, Ireland, was the grandson of the Liberator, Daniel O'Connell. In the early nineteenth century, Dublin was regarded as the second city of the British Empire, but the Irish famine, the Great Hunger (1845–1849), ravaged the country; over one million died and millions emigrated.[1] In the aftermath of this cataclysmic setting, Newman was invited to become the rector of a new Catholic university, where he gave lectures that grew into *The Idea of a University*.[2] Newman once told the poet Gerard Manley Hopkins (who lectured at the Irish University) that if he was not a rector of the university, he would have been a rebel. It is the case that to this day the outstanding legacy of his perspective on education remains within the Irish heart and mentality. This is the view that education is the true key to unlocking the wealth of human persons constituting a people and nation.

In a series of lectures given between 1852 and 1854 and compiled as *The Idea of a University*, Newman managed to explain what a liberal education is and how it is uniquely valuable. In Discourse V, "Knowledge Its Own End," he says, "And now the question is asked of me, What is the *use* of it [knowledge]?"[3] He inquires whether "teaching... carries the attribute of UTILITY along with it."[4] Paradoxically, Newman answers that it is, in fact, "*useless*." Actually, it has no *use* at all, and that is its worth. Knowledge is its own end and not something else. He outlines, "Knowledge is capable of being its own end" and this in turn contributes to us unfolding our nature as persons. This means that "any kind of knowledge, if it really be such, is its own reward."[5] Newman believes it a mistake to burden knowledge unnecessarily "with virtue or religion." It is not the task of education or knowledge "to steel the soul against temptation or to console it in affliction." He argues that "liberal education makes not the Christian, not the Catholic, but the gentleman."[6] So a liberal education "is justified not because it equips us with skills needed to succeed . . . but because it forms the whole person without whom all other achievements lose their value. A human being is an end-in-him-or-herself."[7]

Newman goes into a reflection on what he means by "gentleman." What comes immediately to my mind is Aristotle's term *spoudaios,* which he uses for the mature, spiritual, and rational person.[8] This is the fully realized human person being capable of intelligent thought and responsible decision and action. Newman says the "gentleman" exhibits "a long-sighted prudence" observing the "maxim of the ancient sage, that we should ever conduct ourselves towards the enemy as if he were one day to be our friend."[9] Such a person "knows the weakness of human reason as well as its strength, its province and its limits." Thus, we can see how the human person is central to the Newmanesque perspective on education. Certainly, we need all the help we can get since we cannot gain knowledge "in our sleep, or by haphazard." Newman gives this example: "The best telescope does not dispense with eyes." And so, we cannot dispense with the things we need in order to know but not at the expense of the human person. Persons are ends in themselves. Newman famously says "a University is, according to the usual designation an Alma Mater, knowing her children one by one, not a foundry, or a mint, or a treadmill."[10]

Knowledge is about enlarging the mind and heart.[11] Although Newman admits that if a "practical end must be assigned to a University," he would say it is that of "training good members of society." It is an "art," that is, a way of life. You might find works of genius there but "a University is not a birthplace of poets or of immortal authors." It does not, in fact, promise a generation of "Aristotles or Newtons, of Napoleons or Washingtons, of Raphaels or Shakespeares," though such "miracles of nature do occur within its precincts." No, he says, a university training is "the great ordinary means to a great but ordinary end." It teaches the human person to see "things as they are, to go right to the point." Such a graduate is "at home in any society ... has common ground with every class." He or she knows when to speak and when to be silent. Such a person "is able to listen" and "ask a question pertinently, and gain a lesson seasonably." [12] So a liberal education enables the person to understand who he or she is in relation to the whole order of things. In the end, it is not about the "narcissistic self but about that enlargement of self" which allows us as persons to go beyond ourselves. This means we cannot shy away from "the question of God" as it ultimately concerns the question concerning *who* we are as persons.[13] Newman emphasizes how "religious truth" is "not only a portion, but a condition of general knowledge." To ignore this is "to take the Spring from out of the year."[14]

Person-to-Person[15]

As we see in this chapter, Newman's views on education are not just a theory about a theory but concern students being active participants, not mere spectators in the journey toward universal knowledge. John F. Crosby insightfully notes, "Newman seems to understand things through understanding his own heart; he knows things through the medium of what he himself is." But he is not, of course, a "*what*" but a "*who*." The *who* of *who* we are cannot be reduced to a quantifiable item of knowledge. For Newman, education is about enhancing students' minds and hearts, allowing them to develop "clear-mindedness" and "like-mindedness" as human persons. When he wrote *Apologia Pro Vita Sua* [*A Defense of One's Life*] in response to Charles Kingsley's attack on his character, Newman spells out what was behind his whole life—his desire to live in the truth. Indeed, this fundamental yearning can be understood as what is essential in his educational mission. He says his accuser, Charles Kingsley, asks "What then do I *mean*?" Newman observes how Kingsley asks "not about my words, not about my arguments, not about my actions, as his ultimate point, *but that living intelligence by which I write, and argue, and act.*"[16] Newman says that he understood how in his *Apologia* he must, in fact, "give the true key to my whole life; I must show what I am that it may be seen what I am not.... I wish to be shown as a living man and not as a scarecrow which is dressed up in my clothes."[17]

Newman believes that if we truly want to confront the question about meaning we must face it as living-searching human beings, not just act like dressed-up mannequins clothed in our own words about words or using mere logical argument. Newman holds that the meaning of persons is not contained just in their words but is expressed in *how* they live their life. Indeed, in many of his talks about education, Newman repeatedly brings out the personalist nature of the journey of discovery toward what he calls "universal knowledge." He believes that an educational system "without the personal influence of teachers upon pupils, is an arctic winter; it will create an ice-bound, petrified, cast-iron" organization and nothing else.[18] It was his conviction that truth is primarily communicated in face-to-face witness; without such a personal relationship we have no existential knowledge. Newman ends *The Idea of a University* saying to students that he is "*but fit to bear witness*" to offer suggestions and express his sentiments in order to throw light upon questions.[19] It is unsurprising that Newman chose the moto *Cor ad cor loquitur* ("Heart speaks to heart") when he was made cardinal because it sums up his whole approach to life and education.

Spiritual Foundations

A key to understanding St. John Henry Newman's thought about teaching is his integrating spiritual vision. As noted earlier, he sees religious truth as "not only a portion, *but a condition of general knowledge.*"[20] The word "religious" here does not have denominational connotations because Newman proposes how, as human beings in the journey of the discovery of knowledge, we search to go beyond the merely "conditioned" to the "unconditional," and this movement is, he suggests, found uniquely in our nature as human persons. Taking onboard that which is "beyond us," and understanding how there are horizons of meaning outside ourselves and acting accordingly, is essential if we want to have a truly liberal education measuring up to the reality of *who* we are.

The neglect of such spiritual foundations affects not only human persons and their existence but also "universal knowledge" itself. If you are not open to other viewpoints that are "beyond" or "transcendent" to us, there is the risk, Newman says, of becoming "bigots and quacks, scorning all principles and reported facts." In this way, you end up easily with the big head syndrome, that is, what Newman calls the "man of one idea; which properly means a man of one science, and of the view, partly true ... partly false, which is all that can proceed out of anything partial."[21] Indeed, it is interesting how the Nobel laureate economist Friedrich Hayek once similarly warned, "The economist who is only an economist is likely to become a nuisance if not a positive danger."[22]

Human persons are in a continual process of *"becoming,"* and so are we in our learning. Newman gives an example of the "eyes of the infant first upon the open world." What babies see at first is a medley of colors that do not form into a whole. It is for them a little like looking on "the wrong side of a tapestry." The "little babe stretches out his arms and fingers, as if to grasp or to fathom the many-coloured vision." The baby very gradually learns "the connexion of part with part." And this is, he says, what we are doing "all through life . . . this is our education."[23] The "human being is a process or a project, and it is up to each one of us to take charge of its development."[24] *Who* we are is not yet completed. We are our own artists caught up in the work of "self-creation."

King Charles III (who was then the Prince of Wales) attended Newman's canonization in Rome in 2019. In an editorial of *L'Osservatore Romano*, he commented that although Newman's thoughts on education were well-known, his work on behalf of the poor and children is often forgotten. The king remarked on the new saint's "commitment to ensuring those of all backgrounds shared the opportunities learning can bring."[25] Newman, in fact, spent most of his life in Birmingham, England ministering "by constantly doing . . . duty in the poor-house and gaol of Birmingham."[26] It was truly the case that his heart certainly spoke to the hearts of others.

Four

Søren Kierkegaard (1813–1855): Stages on Life's Way

An Imperative of Living

Søren Aabye Kierkegaard spent most of his life in Copenhagen, Denmark, traveling only on a few occasions to Berlin and Sweden. His interests and writings covered a wide area—philosophy, theology, psychology, literary criticism, religious literature, and fiction. In some of his writings he used funny pseudonyms, like Anti-Climacus, Father Taciturnus, Johannes De Silentio, and Hilarius Bookbinder. This was not just a sign of a certain quirkiness; rather, Kierkegaard's indirect method encouraged readers to participate in his reflective journeys and take on personal responsibility. He felt, "As soon as a person can be brought to stand at the crossroads in such a way that there is no way out for him except to choose, he will choose the right thing."[1] In Kierkegaard's eyes, it is the "choice" of the "choice" which is important, since it is in the choosing that the person "declares itself in its inner infinity and in turn the personality is thereby consolidated."[2] He urges his readers to give preference "not to the activity of thinking" but "to earnestness of spirit." Without doing this, Kierkegaard says, there is the risk of missing out on "the highest, on the only thing that truly gives life meaning." Otherwise, "You may win the whole world but lose yourself."[3] He observed that in human life it is sad that so many people "live out their lives in quiet lostness. . . . They live, as it were, far from themselves and vanish like shadows." They are already dead before they die.[4]

Kierkegaard saw that the fundamental challenge in life lies not in "What am I to know?" but *"What am I to do?"* He says, "The thing is to find a truth which is true *for me*, to find *the idea for which I can live or die."* He asks, for instance, what good is it being able to explain the meaning of Christianity if at the same time it has "*no* deeper significance *for me and for my life*"?[5] The "imperative," he argues, is not in just understanding, but in living. Indeed, he describes how his soul ached for this "as the African desert thirsts for water." Sometimes, he says, a bit like the ancient Greek mathematician, we look for "that Archimedean point" or "fulcrum" on which we can save the whole world. But it is not to be found. That point, if it is to be actually located "must lie outside the world, outside the limitations of time and space."[6] Kierkegaard admits that in his own life he simply found "distraction in outward change." What he lacked is what he needed "*to lead a complete life* and not merely one of understanding." What he searched for was to be "grafted upon the divine" to hold fast to it "even though the whole world" may fall apart. He admits that "*is what I lack and that is what I am striving after.*"[7] Kierkegaard discovers, "It is the divine side of man, his inward action which means everything, not a mass of information.... I have looked in vain for an anchorage in the boundless sea of pleasure and in the depth of understanding."[8]

At a walking trail in Gilbjerg Hoved, Denmark, there stands a memorial stone to Kierkegaard. In this beautiful area, he often enjoyed sitting and being inspired by the whole landscape. In a journal entry for July 29, 1835, he notes:

> The birds sang their evening prayer.... I felt so content in their midst, I rested in their embrace... and I turned back with a heavy heart to mix in the busy world, yet without forgetting such blessed moments.... [I] saw everything as a whole and was strengthened to un-

derstand things differently, to admit how often I had blundered, and [failed] to forgive others.... I stood there alone... and the power of the sea reminded me of my own nothingness, and on the other hand the sure flight of the birds recalled the words spoken by Christ: Not a sparrow shall fall to the ground without your Father: then all at once I felt how great and how small I was.[9]

Stages on Life's Way

Kierkegaard viewed life as being like a dialectical progression through different stages, which he calls "existence-spheres." The first is the esthetic, secondly there is the ethical, and finally you have the religious dimension. He explains, for example, "There is no human being who exists metaphysically."[10] In saying this, he was not denying the importance of studying the nature of reality beyond what we can only see. But he argues that when "being" exists "it does so in the esthetic, in the ethical ... [and] the religious" dimensions of existence. He outlines how "the esthetic is the sphere of *immediacy*, the ethical the sphere of *requirement* ... the religious the sphere of *fulfillment*."[11]

Each stage is characterized by different experiences that are all part of the unfolding of *who* we are as human beings. Throughout his writings, Kierkegaard emphasizes the primacy of the "person." He clearly says, "*Only the person ... acts*, and *only the person* who is repentance exhausts the dialectical, only he *repents*."[12] Thus, we can say that "nothing can contain the person who contains all." Although this is not often fully recognized, personalism definitely has its roots in his thought.[13] In the esthetic dimension, we can remain immersed in sensuous experiences in which we may end up valuing possibilities over reality and, so, remain closed in on ourselves. In the ethical dimension, we act according to expected social norms. But at the same time, we know there are duties and responsibilities that are motivated by truths that lie far beyond what may be considered as societal mores. Kierkegaard outlines and "thoroughly elaborates the interior movement by which in grasping the universality of the ethical life" the human person "gains a foothold in the eternal."[14] This is Kierkegaard's unique insight into the realization that when human persons make "a lifetime commitment" as in an ethical choice, we become more than we are. There is a "becoming" in this which is a going "beyond the self."[15]

A "Knight of Faith" in The Darkness

In *Fear and Trembling*, Kierkegaard gives the example of Abraham's action in the potential sacrificing of his son Isaac. In fact, there is need, he says, of a "new category for understanding Abraham" and his actions. In the case of Abraham, Kierkegaard believes that everything is different because "in his action, he overstepped the ethical altogether." Here he says, "The temptation is the ethical itself which would keep [Abraham] from doing God's will."[16]

So Kierkegaard asks, "How did Abraham exist" and live his life? He explains, "He had faith. That is the paradox that keeps him at the extremity . . . for the paradox is that he puts himself as the single individual in an absolute relation to the absolute. . . . [I]f he is the paradox it is not by virtue of being anything universal, but of being the particular."[17]

By his actions, Abraham places himself in direct relation to God. In this way, we catch a glimpse that the "God relationship is the horizon of the person"; in the end, God is the measure of *who* we are as human persons. This is a clear turnaround from the proposal, made by the Greek Sophist Protagoras in his book *Truth*, that "man is the measure of all things." David Walsh's insights on Kierkegaard are, I believe, invaluable here. He describes how Abraham's sacrifice story "brought the God relationship into focus because it departed so radically from the ethical universal."[18] The story of Abraham and his son in the land of Moriah (Genesis 22) is, according to Kierkegaard, either that of a murderer or else we are moved by "the paradox which is higher than all meditation." Abraham is called a "knight of faith" because we discover in him how the single individual becomes higher than the universal. This means that individuals determine their relation to the universal through their relation to the absolute. We cannot live solely by duty in trying to solve life's challenges. In Abraham's actions there is a going beyond the ethical, that is, actions that are measured merely by societal norms or duties. Therefore, we can see how the ethical is also a passageway to the transcendent and, strangely, whoever walks on the "narrow path of faith" like Abraham cannot be advised what to do or even necessarily understood.

Faith, therefore, is "a marvel, and yet no human being is excluded from it."[19] Prior to faith, Kierkegaard advises, "There is a movement of infinity." And this is the unique drama we see revealed in the story of the sacrifice of Abraham. It is only because of the experience lived that "faith enters" and it is oddly based "on the strength of the absurd." Kierkegaard stresses how only when the individual has exhausted himself or herself in the infinite do they reach "the point where faith can emerge."[20] Walsh remarks how the case of Abraham fascinated Kierkegaard for very good reasons. Kierkegaard saw how Abraham "exemplified the pure inwardness of the God relation" which we cannot necessarily perceive. Very strangely to us, God orders Abraham to go against the law or mores. And Abraham becomes the "knight of faith," holding fast to the call that he alone could hear. Indeed, if Abraham were asked to explain his intentions and actions, he probably could not do so. But he could say that faith is not about "a holding of beliefs, of propositions" but entails a relationship with the "Other" who is beyond us. To know God is not to understand him only through revelational contents but, as John Henry Newman suggests, being in relation with Him "heart-to-Heart." Thus, in essence, faith is "that heart knowledge" and experience.[21]

The Hidden Key: The Neighbor

In Kierkegaard's perspective there lies a hidden key whereby we can reach toward the eternal and so unfold the religious sphere of our existence. He sees the neighbor as the narrow pass or door giving us access to the transcendent. The *neighbor,* Kierkegaard says, is "actually the redoubling of your own self; 'the neighbor' is what thinkers call 'the other,' that by which the selfishness in self-love is to be tested." He describes how the neighbor "is nearer to you than you are to yourself." Even if someone on a desert island lived the new commandment, "You shall love your neighbor as yourself," they could be said to love the neighbor. By loving another person, we can love all. Kierkegaard observes, "If there is one other person whom you love in a Christian sense *as yourself* or in whom you love *the neighbor,* then you love all people."[22] This is what we can call the "multiplier effect." As human beings, we can be and are "like God only in loving."[23]

Kierkegaard readily admits that differences exist between us as human beings. This is reality. Considering our theme in *Myself as Another,* there is no doubt that the "other" is definitely "other" than me. The individual person grows "together with the dissimilarity" that is theirs. In the end, only death forces us to tear these differences away from each other. But if "someone is to truly love his neighbor, it must be kept in mind at all times that his [or her] dissimilarity is a disguise." Christianity does not want to "storm forth to abolish dissimilarity"; instead, it wants "the dissimilarity to hang loosely on the individual, as loosely as the cape the king casts off *to show who he is*, as loosely as the ragged costume in which a supernatural being has *disguised himself.*" Our challenge is to discern how the "dissimilarity" hangs loosely, discovering how in each person "there continually glimmers that essential other, which is common to all, *the eternal resemblance, the likeness.*" Kierkegaard proclaims, in fact, that "every human being is the neighbor." So that in "being king, beggar, scholar, rich man, poor man, male, female, etc., we are not like each other—therein we are indeed different. But in being the neighbor we are all unconditionally like each other. Dissimilarity is temporality's method of confusing... [what] marks every human being differently, but the *neighbor is eternity's mark—on every human being.*"[24]

The hidden key is that the same watermark can be discovered in each one of us. The other, the neighbor, is "the common watermark, but you see it only by means of eternity's light when it shines through the dissimilarity."[25]

Mary: The "Watermark" of *Who* We Are

When it comes to understanding the Virgin Mary, Kierkegaard offers some beautiful insights into her as a person. His emphasis is on *how* Mary lived. Mary is properly revered, he says, for saying "yes," and at the Annunciation making the choice of God. Indeed, artists throughout the centuries have rightly depicted this singular event.[26] Nonetheless, the beauty and depth of *who* Mary is cannot be contained in writings or works of art. Kierkegaard feels that what is often forgotten is "*the distress, the fear* ... [and] *the paradox*" she lived through. Her "yes" cost her. It was, in the words of Dietrich Bonhoeffer, a "costly grace." She willingly paid for it in living her life as she did. The esthetic cannot contain her, neither can only describing *how* she was the highest and purest of our race. Mary and Joseph, we are told, went up to Bethlehem (Lk 2:4) for the census. They lived within the realities of the required norms (that is, the ethical stage). But, as we know, Mary's life speaks of the "beyond" already here on earth among us. All of this, according to Kierkegaard, is fundamental in understanding Mary's way of life. The angel who "was not an obliging one ... came only to Mary, and no one could understand her." She is not "at all the fine lady sitting in her finery." Kierkegaard reflects, "She needs no worldly admiration, as little as Abraham needs our tears, for she was no heroine and he was no hero.... Both of them became greater than that, *not by any means by being relieved of the distress, the agony, and the paradox, but because of these.*"[27]

Abraham and Mary became greater by means of the "distress and the agony and the paradox" they lived through. The spiritual writer and founder Chiara Lubich interestingly describes how Mary "is *the Desolate*" one. Mary lived her own night of the senses, for example, in the loss of Jesus in the Temple. Lubich explains how Mary "*could no longer see him nor hear his voice; his presence was removed from her motherly love.*"[28] In *The Journals*, Kierkegaard reflects that "just as Christ cried out: my God, my God, why hast thou forsaken me—in the same way the Virgin Mary had to suffer something which humanly corresponded to it. A sword shall pierce through thy own soul—and reveal ... that you are in truth the chosen among women, she who found grace in the sight of God."[29]

Søren Kierkegaard intuits beautifully how "being Mary" means embracing everything negative that we might pass through in the stages of our life. In living the paradox of faith as Mary lived, we too can transform it "through Jesus Forsaken [abandoned on the cross] into love."[30]

Five

Ludwig Wittgenstein (1809–1951): A Personal Odyssey

Shooing the "Fly" Out of the Fly Bottle

Ludwig Wittgenstein was born in Vienna, Austria, into a wealthy industrial family that was well-situated in intellectual and cultural Viennese circles. The *London Times* called his father Karl the "Carnegie of Austria." Wittgenstein began studying aeronautical engineering at Manchester University, England, but his interest in the philosophy of mathematics led him to Cambridge University to study with the famous British philosopher Bertrand Russell. During World War I, while in the trenches, he worked on his book *Tractatus Logico-Philosophicus*. Wittgenstein wrote to Russell from the battlefield, "If I don't see the end of this war I must be prepared for all my work to go to nothing. In that case you must get my manuscript printed whether anyone understands it or not."[1] Indeed, Wittgenstein had great problems finding a publisher and "even a single person who understood it."[2] Russell was helpful enough to write a review which convinced the publisher to eventually publish it. He also wrote an introduction to the English translation explaining that it was a text that "no serious philosopher can afford to neglect."[3] Wittgenstein sees his book's contribution as drawing "a limit to thinking, or rather—not to thinking, but to the expression of thoughts; for, in order to draw a limit to thinking we should have to be able to think both sides of this limit."[4] He believes that a thorough study of language can help us draw these limits.

In *Philosophical Investigations*, published posthumously, Wittgenstein points to the need for humility in making the journey of knowledge. He holds that "philosophy must not interfere in any way with the actual use of language." In fact, for Wittgenstein, "a philosophical problem has the form 'I don't know my way'" about a difficult issue.[5] It is not the business of philosophy "to resolve contradiction by means of mathematical or logico-mathematical discovery." The challenge, he says, is that "we [often] lay down rules, a technique, for playing a game, and then, when we follow the rules, things don't turn out as we had assumed." We must face the fact that it is this "entanglement in our rules" that we want to understand. An open philosophy puts all the cards on the table, neither explaining nor deducing anything. Wittgenstein explains, "Since everything lies open to view, there is nothing to explain. For whatever may be hidden is of no interest to us."[6]

At the same time, Wittgenstein observes, "The aspects of things that are most important for us are [frequently] hidden because of their simplicity and familiarity." In other words, it is right in front of our noses, and we cannot recognize it. And we can easily apply this to our understanding of *who* we are as human beings. Very often "[w]e fail to be struck by what, once seen, is most striking and most powerful."[7] In Wittgenstein's view, we must let go of certain conceptions we might have "of what it means to learn to know."[8] He holds that "the paradox disappears only if we make a radical break with the idea that language always functions in one way. Always serves the same purpose: to convey thoughts—which may be about houses, pains, good and evil, or whatever."[9] In fact, the aim of philosophy, Wittgenstein believes, is *"to show the fly the way out of the fly bottle."*[10] In other words, there is a need to escape from the prison-like iron cage of our own limited reasoning about reality. As we have mentioned, Wittgenstein encourages us to draw the limits of our own thinking. Already in the *Tractatus*, he declared that "the sense of the world must lie outside the world."[11] It is true that Wittgenstein's approach was a very scientific one, but meaning in terms of human life cannot, he attests, be reduced to logic: "It must *show* itself in real, everyday execution."[12] His emphasis is on *showing* and not just *looking*. Wittgenstein insisted that "doing, acting, takes priority over all intellectual understanding and reasoning, in every domain."[13]

In terms of understanding what "knowing" actually is, the Canadian philosopher Bernard Lonergan makes a similar point to Wittgenstein, arguing that knowing is not just the same as looking. Discussing empiricism, Lonergan says we know of the advice to "observe the significant facts," but we can only realize the significance of things "through the occurrence of insights." He suggests that we easily forget this, and people end up fancying that what they know "in judgment is not known in judgment and does not suppose an exercise of understanding." They conclude that it is *"by taking a good look at the 'real' that is 'already' out there now"* that they then 'know.'"[14] But human knowing involves far more than mere gaping at, and Wittgenstein is very aware of this. In a discussion about religion and its relevance, for example, he points out that "Christianity is not based on a historical truth; rather, it offers us a (historical) narrative and says: now believe! But do not believe this narrative with the belief appropriate to a historical narrative, rather: believe, through thick and thin, which can only be as the result of life."[15] On the Resurrection, he says, "Only *love* can believe the Resurrection . . . [and] this can come about only if you no longer rest your weight on the earth but suspend yourself from heaven. Then *everything* will be different and it will be 'no wonder' if you do things that you cannot do now."[16] Indeed, there is, I believe, a certain resonance between this and St. John Paul II's open-eyed perspective in

Fides et Ratio, when he says that "faith and reason are like two wings on which the human spirit rises to contemplation of the truth"—so as Wittgenstein intuits, something more, like faith, is needed.[17]

Language: The "Window" onto *Who* We Are as Persons

Wittgenstein's philosophical project can be understood as a therapeutic attempt at recovering the reality of *who* we are as human beings. Contrary to many critics, he is not interested in analysis for analysis's sake. Some thinkers, often called philosophers of human action, believe that if we carry out an x-ray investigation into action, then the essential characteristics of what it means to be human emerge. Wittgenstein concentrates on how it is through a radical reflection on the use of language, which is a unique action, that human identity is essentially disclosed. Thus, language is a window through which we can recapture the reality and distinctiveness of the human person. At the same time, Wittgenstein is well aware of the difficulty of the whole project. He once described language as being like a landscape which presents us with countless fragments saying that "piecing them together is *too hard* for me, I can only make an imperfect job of it."[18] Nonetheless, he explained how going deeper into things "involves our beginning to think about . . . things in a new way . . . The new way of thinking is what is so hard to establish . . . if we clothe ourselves in a new form of expression, the old problems are discarded with the old garments."[19] The Wittgensteinian approach, of course, was not new. The German philosopher Martin Heidegger once remarked on how the essence of the human person "consists in language." He said "language is the house of Being. In its home man dwells." Heidegger, like Wittgenstein, felt that "philosophy is hounded by the fear that it loses prestige and validity if it is not a science." Such a perspective leads to thinking as being "stranded on dry land." Heidegger considered those "who think" and "create with words... the guardians of this home."[20]

Accordingly, language can be said to be the home in which the human person expresses *who* they are. Wittgenstein was always careful not to assign a single function or definition to language. It is too varied a phenomenon for such an approach. The temptation is to think that thought comes first, which we then put into words. It is important to keep in mind that the human being has "the capacity for speaking because of his [or her] relationship with Being."[21] As we have said, Wittgenstein disagrees totally with the idea that thought comes first in the process of human language. Our reasoning is made possible by our interaction as human beings. It is because we are "brought up in endless conversation" that we have "any thoughts in our head at all." It is "action, inter-action" which is primary.[22] We can end up putting the cart before the horse in our analysis. Wittgenstein constantly cautions us, "Don't [just] think," but examine carefully what the human experience tells us.[23] He gives the example of "the activities that we call 'games.'"[24] In order to understand games, we think perhaps "they must have something that is common to *all.*" But, in fact, we discover how "similarities crop up and disappear... we see a complicated network of similarities overlapping and crisscrossing." Games, explains Wittgenstein, actually form a family. And language does the same. Wittgenstein describes it "as in spinning a thread we twist fibre on fibre. And the strength of the thread resides *not in the fact that some one fibre runs through its whole length*, but in the *overlapping of many fibres.*"[25]

As a consequence, if we think we can understand language, for example, solely by linguistic analysis then we are perhaps not measuring up to the entirety of the reality itself.

The linguistic part is only the descriptive skeletal remains of the totality of the human experience. Wittgenstein essentially understands language as a "refinement . . . [because] in the beginning was the deed."[26] Out of the spontaneous interaction of us as human beings "Language develops and, with it, the whole range of concepts opens out." As mentioned earlier, this is why throughout Wittgenstein's writings we find an insistence on *"the priority of action and practice over thought and theory."*[27]

Helen Keller: "W-A-T-E-R"

Perhaps the most striking experience of a human being apprehending the reality of language is Helen Keller's. In my view, it brings to light a little of what Wittgenstein was reflecting on when it comes to understanding the human capacity for language. Helen as a young child could communicate but then illness left her both deaf and blind. She slowly rediscovered what language entailed with the help of her Irish-born teacher, Anne Sullivan. Helen describes how that came about:

> We walked down the path to the well-house. . . . Someone was drawing water and my teacher placed my hand under the spout. As the cool stream gushed over one hand she spelled into the other the word *water*, first slowly, then rapidly. I stood still, my whole attention fixed on the motions of her fingers. Suddenly I felt a misty consciousness as of something forgotten—a thrill of returning thought; *and somehow the mystery of language was revealed to me.* I knew then that "w-a-t-e-r" meant the wonderful cool something that was flowing over my hand. *That living word awakened my soul, gave it light, hope, joy, set it free!* . . . I left the well-house eager to learn. *Everything had a name, and each name gave birth to a new thought.*[28]

Helen's experience and insight into our unique capacity for language cannot be reached solely by "a semiology of parts" of words and sentences.[29] Human language is not just words about words, since this risks leaving meaning only at the level of the verbal. Wittgenstein argues that when we speak of "understanding a sentence" we see "the sense in which it can be replaced by another." But there is also "the sense in which it cannot be replaced by any other."[30] Thus, in saying "w-a-t-e-r" Helen Keller is not just using a word, she is, in Wittgenstein's terms, "understanding." The material elements themselves do not "trigger the use of language—that requires human subjects [persons] operating in an interpersonal context."[31] For Wittgenstein, language is, therefore, not a private affair; it necessarily involves others.[32] It is a carrier of infinite meaning for others and for me. It witnesses to the "beyond" of experience, which even escapes our meager words. When we speak and talk, we exchange not just know-how or information but the reality of "the incommunicable openness of the self to the other."[33] Knowing myself necessarily involves the other. And we can see this especially in the case of Helen Keller and her teacher Anne Sullivan.[34] Reflecting on language actually pushes us toward the edge of a discovery of *who* we are. Language is the way by which I can say *who* I am as a human being. This is why it is a window through which we can discover and learn the unique nature of our being human persons.[35]

Six

Gabriel Marcel (1889–1973): A Philosopher of "Presence"

A Philosopher on the Mystery of the Person

Gabriel Marcel, a French philosopher, playwright, and composer, belonged to a school of philosophy (personalism) in which the human person is central to its reflections. In *Myself as Another*, we discuss the writings of some members of this school of thought because of their relevance to our theme. Even Pope Francis seems a Marcel fan since he quotes from his *Creative Fidelity* in his encyclical on social friendship, *Fratelli Tutti*. The pope observes how human beings can never fully know themselves; that is, they are a mystery since "apart from an encounter with other persons: 'I communicate effectively with myself only insofar as I communicate with others.'"[1] Many other philosophers and writers were also influenced by Marcel's philosophy.

Jacques Derrida, for instance, who we will discuss in a subsequent chapter, was inspired by Marcel's two-volume *The Mystery of Being*.[2] In those two volumes, Marcel distinguished between a "problem," which exists independently of any individual and can be solved, and a "mystery," which is one's own, and cannot. Derrida was impressed by Marcel's approach that life "*is not a problem to be solved but a mystery to be lived.*"[3] Indeed, as I have said, at the heart of Marcel's *Being and Having* is this distinction between problem and mystery.[4] He sees a problem as something "before us and blocking our way.... Something that ... can be solved by objective, detached, factual knowledge." Whereas, a mystery personally involves us, it is "something that cannot be solved; it can only be participated in."[5] Marcel mentions also how the thoughts of Søren Kierkegaard influenced him, and he feels that he, in some way, accomplished what the Danish philosopher was straining toward.[6] The American philosopher Josiah Royce, who explored similar themes, also inspired Marcel. In his writings, Royce outlined, for example, how "the human Self... is not a Thing... but a Life with Meaning.... If I am any Reality whatever, then I am doing something that nobody else can do.... The uniqueness of my meaning is the one essential fact about me."[7]

Gabriel Marcel taught philosophy at various schools and universities throughout France, but this was interrupted firstly by World War I, during which he directed a service for the Red Cross that sought to find soldiers missing in action. This whole experience marked a turning point in his life. His diaries from around this time show how he refused to treat the lost as just numbers or cases. He "regarded them as real beings who needed his help.... They... filled him with anguish."[8] These war experiences and many other personal sufferings impressed upon him and deepened his conviction "that abstract thought misses the whole drama" of human existence.[9]

Homo Viator

As human beings, Marcel remarked, we are simply *homo viator*, that is, "journeying man" or "wanderers." In a lecture given in Frankfurt, Germany in 1964, he explained how the role of the philosopher is to be a "watchman," that is, a sentinel in this world to *who* we are. He compared his work to that of a mother who wakens her children to feed them. He described how "to awaken, to feed, to teach how to breathe: these essential life-functions have their exact correspondence at the level of philosophy." Philosophy prepares us, he says, "for the ineffable surprise of the eternal tomorrow."[10] He describes himself as "a philosopher of the threshold," since he wants to address those "who seek in the darkness, often in anguish" rather than those who have "an unshakeable faith" and therefore have no need for him. He explains that he has tried to make his philosophical discernment "in the prison in which we find ourselves." It is from the perspective of the prisoner that he has tried to reflect on *who* we are as human persons.[11] Marcel says the main question he must ask himself when his "inner gaze looks at the last twenty years, is the one Arnaud Chartrain asked his mother-in-law, Evelyne," a character in one of his plays: "What are you living on?" Marcel comments that if he were to try and honestly answer this question, he would explain how what sustained him has been "*an invisible support*" and also his family.[12] Life, he holds, is but a preparation "for that life beyond this world whose magnetic pull, too often unsuspected ... alone can make beings, *persons*, of us—souls."[13]

Recollection: A Recapturing *Who* We Are

Since Gabriel Marcel was also a dramatist, poet, and composer, in his writings he very often does not begin "with abstract definitions and dialectical argumentation." These would merely discourage his readers and audience. He prefers to begin with an "intuitive characterization of persons for whom any sense of being or the ontological is lacking." Our world, he believes, is dominated by the notion of function. We can end up considering human beings as "merely an agglomeration of functions."[14] Nonetheless, living is not just about mere existence. Life in a world "centered on function leads to despair because such a world is empty, it rings hollow."[15] This kind of world, Marcel, claims, leaves no room for "mystery." Indeed, to try and eliminate mystery from the drama of human existence leads, he believes, to a "degenerate rationalism."[16] So there is a need for what he calls *"recollection,"* which is "a relaxation, a letting go" involving *"abandoning to . . .* [and] *relaxing in the presence"* of *who* we are. Doing this bears witness to the reality that we are not purely and simply living things. We are not just creatures "thrown into life with no hold on it." [17] Marcel observes how the process of recollection *"does not* [simply] *consist in looking at something,* [rather] *it is a retrieval, a renewal."* This entry into oneself does not mean a purely turning back on ourselves. Rather we are "in the presence of the paradox of mystery whereby the self into which I return ceases,"[18] a mystery that actually involves an emptying of self. St. Paul's statement, "You are not your own" (1 Cor 6:19) best expresses what we are speaking about. And this is true both ontologically and concretely. Marcel speaks of how this gives us an "intuition of being," but it is hard to explain, and this all requires "a movement of conversion" on our part.[19] He holds that in drama, we are better able to grasp more clearly what we are speaking about. That is, the mystery of *who* are as human persons. St. John Paul II as a philosopher, dramatist, and poet was, indeed, of the same mind.[20]

View of Delft

Marcel, as we said, believes that it is in drama, music, and art that "metaphysical thought becomes conscious and defines itself concretely." He sees drama as being like "living tissue" that regenerates life and our understanding of *who* we are. In *The Mystery of Being,* in a discussion on the human person, Marcel gives the example of Johannes Vermeer's painting *View of Delft*. He explains how we, as "being-in-a-situation," can creatively develop.[21] When it comes to understanding *who* we are, there can be no "global abstraction, [nor] any final high terrace to which we can climb by means of abstract thought." In the action of a painter like Vermeer, we can, for example, see disclosed the power of our "inwardness" as persons shine through, in the transformation of our "being-in-a-situation." In the painter's action, we see unveiled the reality that we do not, as persons, remain idle spectators being conditioned by our conditions. Marcel outlines, in fact, how in viewing the painting we realize that "if for Vermeer the view of Delft had been a mere spectacle, if he himself could have been reduced to a mere spectator, he would never have been able to paint his picture." It is in an artwork such as Vermeer's that we can discover the uniqueness of each person's "inwardness." Vermeer did not just paint *View of Delft* as he would another place. Indeed, if he had lived "somewhere else, though he still might have been an artist, he would not have been Vermeer." Marcel describes how it is only when we cease to be mere onlookers and get involved that we discover how we as human beings can *admire* and *contemplate* a painting. In this way we participate in the work of the artist realizing that to admire already means "to create . . . to be receptive in an active, alert manner."[22]

The artist's work can, of course, be analyzed at the level of its being an "object" or a "thing" and as coming from a particular school of art and so exemplifying different artistic methods. But we can also somehow encounter the experience of the artist as a person in the work. Marcel uses the word *encounter* in his philosophy deliberately because he believes that "there cannot be an encounter or a meeting in the fullest sense except between beings endowed with a certain inwardness." In contemplating works of art like Vermeer's painting, we can stand at the threshold of such experiences, not remaining on the outside but entering in. Using the artistic example of Vermeer, Marcel conveys how constitutive of our human nature is the reality that "there is creative development as soon as there is *being in a situation*."[23] Marcel observes, "The true artist does not create for himself alone but for everyone, he is satisfied only if that condition is fulfilled."[24] Thus, the artist also lives out in a way the theme of our book: *Myself as Another*.

"Sickness unto Death": "You" Will Never Die

In terms of his philosophical approach, Marcel is often called an existentialist. But he would not easily agree to such a label. Indeed, his reflections on human mortality surely shatter any such simplistic categorization. Gabriel Marcel's mother died when he was young, and then the early deaths of his wife and other family members through illness deeply affected him. Death, in a way, truly tests how we experience and understand "presence" and the "other." Marcel once described it as the "springboard of an absolute hope." Paul Ricoeur, interviewing Marcel on the role of drama in his work, observes how "death is truly the crisis which completely shatters all faith in existence, all certitude of presence." In his plays, Marcel often takes up these themes, but critics often complain that his work deals too much with sickness and death. Marcel replied, "I do not think that we can give too much importance to sickness and death." It is in "facing them, in fact, that we are at the very heart of our destiny and of our mystery."[25]

Reading about the death of someone in a newspaper is often nothing more than an object of notification. But when it comes to a human person we love and "*who has been given to me as a presence;*" it is in the experience of a death like this that we are speaking of how to hold on to that presence. Marcel explains how the presence of a person is a reality. It is not a concept or "a mere effigy." It involves us in living a creative fidelity of relation with another person. Person is relation, and living this truth means that we actively maintain ourselves in what Marcel calls "a state of permeability."[26] We are reminded here of the Johannine "I in them and thou in me" (Jn 17:23). This indicates that I cannot treat "the other as if he or she were simply placed there, positioned in front of me." There arises "between the other and me a relationship which in a certain sense goes way beyond the conscious awareness I may have of it." Marcel holds that the "*other person is not only before me, the other is also within me.*" The purely physical categories are totally transcended. He outlines how in the death of a loved one, "*even when I can neither touch you nor see you, I feel it, you are with me.*" It would be a complete betrayal of *who* you are as a person "not to be assured of this."[27]

Marcel describes how in experiencing the death of those we love, we can recapture the truth of reality. In these situations, we face ultimate realities. There is, in fact, no such thing as death in general. It is encountered close to us and not as an abstraction. The death of friends and relatives is "within reach of our spiritual sight." If we, for example, keep vigil at the bedside of a loved one who is dying, what are we communicating in our care and solicitude for them? Marcel remarks that "to love a being [a human person] . . . is to say *you, you in particular, will never die.*"[28] He says that if we consent to the death of a *person as person*, we give him or her up to death. But to say that I love you means that that love will never die. It is experienced in a new way, that is, in the presence of *God who is Love*. Our human experiences are transitory and fleeting, but in God's presence, we behold and experience God's unconditional love for eternity. Thus, "the one who loves, reigns. This is the way it is." The reason for this is that those "who love, give. Always give. And their giving makes them regal, and they have within a fullness that has no end."[29] To say that the "tenderly loved being [person] no longer exists" is a betrayal of such love.[30] As human persons, we are embodied beings, but we are not thereby entombed. As Jesus says, God is of the living and not the dead since "for him all are alive." Marcel observes that for Christians, "death compared with life represents not less but more.... It is an exaltation."³¹ In light of this, we are challenged to live fully alive and not go around as if we are half-dead. There is an Irish saying appropriate at this point. It says of those who have died: "The candle is quenched only because a new day has dawned." This is why, perhaps, in *Homo Viator* Marcel spoke of being "a philosopher of the threshold."³² In his poem, "Spirit of Metamorphosis," he pleads:

> When we try to push back the veil of clouds
> which separates us from the other realm,
> guide our novice gesture!
> And when the appointed hour chimes, awaken in us
> the light-hearted spirit of the traveler, who fastens on his sack,
> while outside the misted windows there appears
> the gentle dawning of daybreak!³³

Seven

Edith Stein (1891–1942): Stairway to the "Other"

Let Us Go for Our People

Before Edith Stein perished along with her sister Rosa at Auschwitz concentration camp in Poland in 1942, she lived life as a professional philosopher. She and her sister grew up in a Jewish household. She is known for her work in the field of phenomenology and was a student of Edmund Husserl in Göttingen, Germany. Without being aware of it, Husserl was "founding an intellectual movement that eventually would result in the conversion of many of the students to Christianity," including Edith Stein herself.[1] She became very friendly with many other philosophers, but especially with Hedwig Conrad-Martius and her husband Theodor. While at their house, when her hosts were out, Edith came across the autobiography of Teresa of Avila in the library. Once she started reading it, she could not put it down, saying to herself "This is the truth." What she discovered in the autobiography of Saint Teresa confirmed her own experience. It was that "*God is not a God of knowledge, God is love. He does not reveal his mysteries to the deductive intelligence, but to the heart that surrenders to him.*"[2] Edith Stein was baptized a Roman Catholic on January 1, 1922, and her godmother was a Lutheran, Hedwig Conrad-Martius. Her sister Rosa would also later convert. Stein entered a Carmelite convent in Cologne, Germany, but because of Nazi persecution of those of Jewish birth, she had to flee to an abbey in Echt, Holland. Rosa ended up joining her sister there too, and from the abbey in Echt, they were both finally transported to Auschwitz. On August 2, 1942, the SS arrested Edith, Rosa, and many others in retaliation for the Catholic bishops' letter of protest against the persecution of the Jews being read out publicly in all the churches.[3] Part of the Dutch bishops' pastoral letter read: "Are we not, after all, partly responsible for the disasters that affect us? Have we always fulfilled the duties of justice and charity toward our neighbor?" When the Nazis came to the Carmelite convent in Echt to arrest the sisters because of their Jewish background, Edith is reported to have said, "Come Rosa. We're going for our people." When you inquire into Edith Stein's life you can see that her attitude and approach were not a once-off reaction. In fact, her whole life and intellectual study were a preparation for these consequential moments in going "beyond" herself. In a letter to one of the sisters in the convent in Cologne where she had formerly lived, she wrote, "It is faith in our hidden stories that ought to console us when what we see externally in ourselves and in others tends to depress us."[4]

Making Ourselves One with the "Other:" Empathy

Besides being a saint and a martyr, Stein was, as I said, a philosopher of the human person. Among many other things, she studied what in philosophy is called the problem of "empathy" [*Einfühlung*]. Her doctoral dissertation, *On the Problem of Empathy*, was directed by Edmund Husserl.[5] At the end of that work she wrote, "This is how *empathy and inner perception* work hand in hand *to give me myself to myself.*"[6] As we can see, this is in line with our theme in *Myself as Another*. In its most basic sense, empathy is a way in which we can experience other "experiencing subjects," that is, human beings who present themselves to us as they face moments of happiness, sorrow, or anger. Stein focused primarily on the "*how*" and "what" that happens when human beings empathize with one another in such situations. Is it really possible for us to empathize with each other and to communicate about it? When I "empathize" with someone, am I just saying: "I know or imagine what your pain is like," which is *a theory of imitation or imagination*? Or if I say, "I see how upset you are," am I identifying with this because I remember what feeling annoyed is like, which is *a theory of association*? Or is John Stuart Mill correct, that is, although there is outer and inner evidence, as when a person is obviously grieving, we can only "get at the facts" of the matter by means of inference, which is *a logical theory*. Stein's *On the Problem of Empathy* analyzes in depth these various theories of empathy.[7]

As we can see, these theoretical explanations can remain somewhat superficial. Stein outlines her unhappiness with them in her doctoral studies. For her, the truth did not "exist as an abstraction." It is "something incarnated in persons" and is therefore totally "inconceivable apart from love."[8] Indeed, our own "lived experiences" of such situations leave us equally unhappy with such abstract accounts. They do not really explain what we are doing when we empathize with someone who is bereaved, sick, or maybe in trouble. We can think here of our own experiences of caring for family members or friends who are ill or in need of our support. Stein believed that a thoroughgoing analysis of the experiences involved in "empathetic awareness" can show us *who we really are as human beings*. She outlines how we, in fact, possess a unique capacity for placing ourselves into the situation of the "other." Chiara Lubich speaks of the "art of loving," a central point of which is "making ourselves one" with the "other." She writes, "Knowing how to make yourself one" with others means "making your own their burdens, their thoughts, their sufferings, their joys."[9] Is this really possible, we may well ask? In her investigations, as we have previously remarked, Edith Stein used a philosophical method known as phenomenology, which tries to get to the experience *in itself*. The approach is to "x-ray" human actions and experiences like empathy and so disclose the essential nature of being a person.

Stein's exploration into empathy thereby becomes a way of unfurling *who* we are as human beings. She shows how empathy is essentially an act of self-transcendence, that is, of going beyond ourselves, and so entering the other, becoming directly aware of them through their thoughts and feelings. This is *who* we are as persons. To empathize, therefore, is a profoundly human act. I can actually place myself in the shoes of the other, and in so doing, I also *become who* I am. It is an act of "self-creation." It signifies being faithful to *who* we are as human beings. This means that the joy, grief, or anger of the other can be an object of my direct awareness and experience. It is, as she says, "immediately given, not mediated by its expression or by bodily appearances."[10] Amazingly, we can become aware of the experience of the other in its originality. Grief makes itself directly present in the other for me. We are not just dealing with a representation, a simulation, or an appearance of the experience when we empathize. In the neighbor who is grieving, sorrow gives itself immediately to me. It is, therefore, a way for communion between persons, and any understanding of this cannot merely remain at the level of description.

When Stein was writing on this theme, many other philosophers simply remained at a descriptive stage, forgetting the essential human significance of the action. It is important to keep in mind that she focused on empathy, not for its own sake but because she saw it as a way in which human beings actually communicate with each other. What interested her most was exploring the "possibility of mutual communication," that is, "the possibility of establishing community." It turns out that her investigation into empathy, although limited, unlocks our overall understanding of the nature of human persons. As human beings we can truly go beyond our outer shell and enter into the *who* of the other. At the same time, because we are unrepeatable as human beings, each person's happiness, sorrow, or anger is unique; nevertheless, we can enter into someone else's life experience.

In the Shoes of the "Other"

Edith Stein knew well what she was talking about because of her experiences as a military nurse's aide. As a volunteer with the Red Cross during World War I, Stein and others inhabited a dystopian landscape in which most were but sleepwalkers moving toward the cataclysmic catastrophe of the Great War, which brought about the deforestation of what it means to be human beings.[11] Stein initially wanted to help at the frontlines, but she ended up in Austria nursing wounded soldiers. She relates many experiences in her autobiography, *Life in a Jewish Family*.[12] She observes how some of the nurses, although they "carried out their duties capably and diligently," were "more motivated by ambition than by a love for humanity." The doctors and nurses liked her since she lived her life empathetically. She says, "I cheerfully accepted any kind of duty entrusted to me and was always happy to substitute for the others."[13] She was surely living out empathy. She did not just skate over these encounters with patients and staff. While nursing soldiers, she first saw and experienced another human being die in front of her. She relates how when she was collecting the dead soldier's few belongings, a piece of paper from his wife fell out of the man's notebook, "a prayer for the preservation of his life. Only when I saw it did I fully realize what this death meant, humanly speaking. . . . I pulled myself together and went to call the doctor."[14]

At another point, Stein relates how the severely ill men often asked whether she would be returning to see and care for them the next day. When she told them that she would, they were delighted; this was "the first sign" that these men "of sorrows found my care a blessing."[15] She was able to write about empathy as she did because of her empathetic awareness of the pain, grief, and anger of the wounded. Stein's experiences reveal empathy disclosed as a lived reality, not merely a problem or intellectual abstraction to be solved. She did not see difficulties in terms of resolving them, but to be loved empathetically, unfolding in lives lived for the other. It turns out that placing ourselves in the shoes of others is a stairway that leads to a greater understanding and living the truth of being human persons.

Edith Stein did not become a saint in Auschwitz; she was already a person who lived out the "priority of the other." In the site of greatest darkness, she became a crossing point in love for God and others. *Who* the other is cannot be encapsulated in definitions or abstractions. The human person cannot be a "proposition." At her canonization, St. John Paul II said,

> [She] traveled the arduous path of philosophy with passionate enthusiasm. Eventually she was rewarded: she seized the truth. Or better: she was seized by it. Then she discovered that truth had a name: Jesus Christ. From that moment on, the incarnate Word was her One and All. . . .
>
> *Pay attention! Your life is not an endless series of open doors!* Listen to your heart! Do not stay on the surface, but *go to the heart of things!* And when the time is right, have the courage to decide! The Lord is waiting for you to put your freedom in his good hands.[16]

Unfinished Coda

Throughout T.S. Eliot's "Four Quartets" a refrain recurs: "In my beginning is my end." In "The Dry Salvages" he describes

> the point of intersection of the timeless
> With time, is an occupation of the saint—
> No occupation either, in a lifetime's death in love,
> Ardour and selflessness and self-surrender.[17]

As I mentioned, Edith Stein did not become a saint only in the tragedy of Auschwitz, since her "end" was also her "beginning"! She already lived the "new saintliness" that Emmanuel Levinas spoke of, that is, the "priority of the other." To discover this, I suggest that we also need to dig deep down, for example, into her *Self-Portrait in Letters 1916–1942*.[18] Stitched into these letters are her way of beginning again with each person. To her, no one is a lost cause, not even Edmund Husserl, whom she always called "the Master." She failed to gain a permanent academic position in university and so ended up as a high school teacher. Husserl and Heidegger claimed that they could do nothing to assist her. If the truth be told, they gave in to the academic and national politics of the times! But you can read about Stein's reactions to this suffering in her letters. To Fritz Kaufmann she writes, "I am no longer the least bit furious or sad. Instead I find the whole matter very funny. After all, I do not consider life on the whole to carry so much weight that it would matter a great deal what position I occupy. And I would like you [Kaufmann] to make that attitude your own."[19]

She lived this particularly in terms of her constancy as a friend and reaching out to others. To her, everyone was a candidate for the splendor and truth of our being human, which is not just finite but infinite. Stein's writings are a storehouse because they attempt to get to the heart of what it means to be a person. But her breakthroughs are found at times in between the lines. She intuited, in fact, how Husserl's analysis, although insightful, focused on the "particular" [consciousness] as being the "whole." And consciousness is not the totality, but an expression of *who* we are as human persons.

As Husserl was on his deathbed, Edith Stein remarked in a letter, "As regards the Master [Husserl], I have no worries about him. To me it has always seemed strange that God could restrict his mercy to the boundaries of the visible Church. God is truth and whoever seeks the truth is seeking God, whether he knows it or not."[20]

Toward the close of his life, Husserl experienced attraction to Christ, which for years had lain buried under philosophical problems. Stein notes, "On Good Friday, his [Husserl's] first words were, 'Good Friday! What a wonderful day. Christ has forgiven us everything.'"[21]

In a letter dated February 12, 1928, addressed to a sister in Speyer, Cologne, Germany, Edith Stein describes how gradually, "I realized that something else is asked of us in the world and that, even in the contemplative life, one may not sever connection with the world. I even believe that the deeper one is drawn into God, *the more one must 'go out of oneself;' that is, one must go to the world in order to carry the divine life into it.*"[22]

Eight

Viktor Frankl (1905–1997): A Why to Live For

An Ascent

There is no doubt that forced isolation involves a great cost at both a personal and a societal level. Already in the fourth century BC, Aristotle had the essential insight that our nature as human beings is social. In Genesis, we read, "It is not good that the man should be alone" (2:18). During the international pandemic, the greatest prison we lived in was separation from our family and friends. But even during this untold human suffering, new horizons of meaning emerged. Aleksandr Solzhenitsyn, who experienced eight years in a Communist gulag, acknowledges that a lack of freedom leads to a spiraling descent of the human spirit, but there can be "the ascent." The way down can lead upward. Solzhenitsyn says: "your soul, which was formerly dry, now ripens from suffering."[1]

Viktor Frankl, the Austrian psychiatrist and philosopher who wrote *Man's Search for Meaning*, indicates some useful signposts to help us cross whatever strange landscape we find ourselves inhabiting.[2] In 1942, Frankl and his family were arrested and deported. The manuscript of an unfinished book he had carefully sewn into the lining of his coat was eventually found and confiscated. He spent time in Auschwitz, Dachau, and other concentration camps. His parents, brother, and pregnant wife all died in the camps. While in prison, Frankl worked on recreating his book on bits of paper. Afterward, he wrote several more books, including *The Will to Meaning*, *The Unheard Cry for Mean-*

ing, *The Unconscious God, Psychotherapy and Existentialism*, and *Man's Search for Ultimate Meaning*. More recently, *Yes to Life: In Spite of Everything* was published. Having gone through life in the prison camps, he understood that to restore a human being's inner strength, those persons had first to be shown some future purpose. Frankl explained,

> Any attempt to restore man's inner strength in the camp had first to succeed in showing him some future goal. Nietzsche's words, "He who has a *why* to live for can bear almost any *how*," could be a guiding motto.... We needed to stop asking of ourselves as those who were being questioned by life.... Our answer must consist not in talk... but in right action and conduct. Life ultimately means [that is, our ultimate end is] taking responsibility to find the right answer to its problems and to fulfill the tasks which it constantly sets for each individual.[3]

A Meaning of Meaning

Frankl observed how prisoners lived through certain stages of existence. Initially, there was "shock," an early loss of identity with a "delusion of reprieve." Then there was "apathy," which the prisoner experienced as an "emotional death." The prisoner is dead to himself and to others. All of this leads to an experience of "depersonalization," which the prisoner experiences as a kind of aftershock. These men had been "*depersoned*" through their harrowing experiences and "only slowly could... [they] be guided back to the... truth" of who they are as human persons.[4]

But Frankl relates a personal experience he had a few days after liberation. He describes:

> I walked through the country past flowering meadows.... Larks rose to the sky and I could hear joyous

singing.... I stopped, looked around, and up to the sky—and then I went down on my knees. At that moment there was very little I knew of myself or of the world—I had but one sentence in mind—always the same: "I called to the Lord from my narrow prison and He answered me in the freedom of space.".... I know that on that day, in that hour my new life started. Step for step I progressed, until I again became a human being.[5]

Obviously, we can go backward on the personal, societal, and economic levels. In other words, we can easily lose what it means "to be" a human person, and this is very much evidenced in the first part of Frankl's book on the experiences in the camps. It became possible, he says, to lose the "innerhold" of what it means for us "to be." It is true to say that we "become" *who* we are as human persons. But we can also "unbecome" *who* we are as human beings. In *Man's Search for Meaning*, I believe, we are presented not only with an investigative analysis of human nature, but there is also a curative aspect involving the recovery of the originary truth of what it means to be a human being.

Notwithstanding the cataclysmic crucible of human suffering Frankl and the prisoners went through, he outlines the hidden roots, that is, the emergent essential realities making up *who* we are. These are not just theoretical abstractions; they are part of our reality as human beings. In living, we unfold *who* we are, and what is more, we can also recapture our personhood should we become disordered and depersonalized. Frankl admits that his psychological analysis might just lead us all to utter despair! He acknowledges, "I may give the impression that the human being is completely and unavoidably influenced by his surroundings."[6] But this need not be the case.

Recapturing Who We Are

Viktor Frankl outlines how "everything *can be taken from a man but one thing*: the last of the human freedoms—*to choose one's attitude in any given set of circumstances, to choose one's own way*."[7] Frankl's vital insight is that we can be "inwardly free" while being outwardly constrained. In *Man's Search for Meaning*, we discover the emergence of a philosophy of human action, that is, of the "will" and "becoming." As Frankl clearly describes,

> *There were always choices to make.* Every day, every hour, offered the opportunity to make a decision, a decision which determined whether you would or would not submit to those powers which threatened *to rob you of your very self, your inner freedom*, which determined whether or not you would *become the plaything of circumstance*, renouncing freedom and dignity to become molded into the form of the typical inmate.[8]

Frankl basically sees the human person as key to our quest in recapturing meaning. He says the significance we give to existence "has a bearing on creative work as much as it does on human love. When the impossibility of replacing a person is realized, it allows the responsibility which man has for his existence and its continuance to appear in all its magnitude.... He knows the 'why' for his existence and will be able to bear almost any 'how.'"[9] Frankl coins the term "logotherapy" for his approach. The attitude is that human persons recover *who* they are through finding a sense of existential meaning. It is about regaining meaning in life. Life, he says, "consists in fulfilling a meaning, rather than in the mere gratification and satisfaction of drives and instincts."[10]

But what is the meaning Frankl speaks about, and how can we recover it in our lives? According to him, there are three ways in which we can recapture existential meaning. These are: "(1) by creating a work or doing a deed; (2) by experiencing something or encountering someone; and (3) by the attitude we take to unavoidable suffering."[11] These are the often-hidden roots in recapturing *who* we are as human persons. How can being creative answer *who* I am as a human being? We must realize that we are not just rational beings, but we have a "doer" nature too. My mind grounds "doing" as well as "knowing." Frankl, for example, remarks on the experience of "*give-up-itis*" he observed among some prisoners.[12] They "unbecome" *who* they are as persons. They stop "doing" and so they stop "being." He explains how "nothing... could induce them to change their minds.... Meaning orientation had subsided" and vanished from them.[13] We have the capacity to know the good, but we equally have the power to be and do good. In doing the deed, we *become* good.

Hence, the first way of recovering meaning is being "creative," and this emerges especially during times of crisis like the recent pandemic. Throughout it all, this was most evident in the examples of medics, businesspeople, and even artists who searched for new ways to provide for us and communicate with our souls. I recall the wonderful news reports of musicians and singers in Italy putting on impromptu performances from their home balconies for their families and neighbors. This is not perhaps so surprising since an artist, after all, cannot but be *who* he or she is. Speaking about art, Pope Francis says it has "in itself a salvific dimension" being open to all and everyone and "offering consolation and hope to each one."[14] Art's creativity "knows how to speak to persons" but our normal human deeds also have this capacity. In creating a work or doing a deed we transform not just external objects or our environment but our inner selves. In an amazing way, we become *who* we are in human action, and this is what gives work its dignity.

The second way we can discover the meaning of our existence is by "experiencing something or encountering someone." Frankl is speaking not of experiencing an object or having a possession. He explains how in experiencing "goodness, truth and beauty" we can grasp significant meaning. Traditionally, "goodness, truth, and beauty" are called the "transcendentals." Each of the transcendentals goes beyond the limitations of place and time and is rooted in "being." Frankl remarks that "we who lived in concentration camps can remember the men who walked through the huts comforting others, giving away their last piece of bread."[15] This is the face-to-face encounter with "goodness" evidenced in the lives of others, an experience that cannot be taken away from us. It is, as Frankl says, "the last of the human freedoms—to choose one's attitude in any given set of circumstances." During the [virus] epidemic and "lockdown" we too can recall the many heroic stories of such decisions of goodness lived by nurses, doctors, chaplains, and hospital staff accompanying patients who were dying alone, without friends or relatives at their bedsides.

Thus, Frankl believes that in encountering another person we can recapture what it is *to be who* we are. This is love not in the abstract, but it means to love "some—one." He says we come to meaning "by experiencing another human being in his very uniqueness—by loving him." Frankl explains,

> Love is the only way to grasp another human being in the innermost core of his personality. No one can become fully aware of the very essence of another human being unless he loves him. By his love he is enabled to see the essential traits and features in the beloved person; and even more, he sees that which is potential in him, which is not yet actualized. Furthermore, by his love the loving person enables the beloved person to actualize these potentialities.[16]

So, in "love" we actualize *who* we are as human beings.

I love, therefore, I Am

If Descartes said, "I think, therefore, I am," we can say, "I love, therefore, I am." We do not have to be physically present to do this, and today's digital world provides various ways of communicating our practical love and care for others. Frankl describes how in the concentration camps he discovered "how a man who has nothing left in this world may still know bliss." There is the discovery that "love goes far beyond the physical person of the beloved. It finds its deeper meaning in his spiritual being, his inner self." We are reminded here perhaps of St. Augustine's experience when he said, "late have I loved you, beauty so old and so new: late have I loved you. And see, you were within and I was in the external world and sought you there...You were with me, and I was not with you."[17]

The third way we have of recapturing meaning as persons, according to Frankl, is "by the attitude we take to unavoidable suffering."[18] In the fifth century BC, the Greek tragedians spoke of the principle of *"pathei mathos,"* that is, the fact that real wisdom often comes through suffering. Frankl says that when we discover that external circumstances cannot be changed, "what then matters is to bear witness to the uniquely human potential at its best, which is to transform a personal tragedy into a triumph, to turn one's predicament into a human achievement. When we are no longer able to change a situation ... we are challenged to change ourselves."[19]

Viktor Frankl freely admits that in some situations we are cut off from the opportunity "to do one's work or to enjoy one's life." There is the "unavoidability of suffering"; but in accepting this bravely, "life has a meaning up to the last moment, and it retains this meaning literally to the end." The attitude we take of loving "Love" itself is transformative, helping us go beyond our limitations. Chiara Lubich says *this secret way of living is a "person,"* namely, *Jesus Forsaken*. He is the very reason "why persons can be fulfilled, [in] going beyond any limitation."[20] And this gives us a "why" to live for.

Nine

Hannah Arendt (1906–1975): New Beginnings

Early Stages

Political philosopher and Holocaust survivor Hannah Arendt was born into a German-Jewish family. After high school, she attended Marburg University, where she became a student of the philosopher Martin Heidegger and had a short love affair with him. She then moved to Heidelberg University, where she completed her doctorate on "The Concept of Love in St. Augustine" under the philosopher Karl Jaspers. Her favorite passage from Augustine was taken from the *Confessions*. She observed how, reflecting on what it means to lose a friend who died, Augustine "became a question to himself" because of the loss. Arendt quotes how after "the loss of life of the dying" followed "the death of the living."[1] Indeed, throughout her writings, she continually examines how we as human persons are like cyphers needing continual decoding. The human being is not some abstract static notion but is uniquely personified or even "de-personified" in each one of us. This emerges clearly in one of her most famous and controversial writings concerning the trial of the Nazi leader Adolf Eichmann. These appeared initially as articles in *The New Yorker* and were eventually published as *Eichmann in Jerusalem: A Report on the Banality of Evil*.[2]

The Politics of the Person

What I find most revelatory about Hannah Arendt are not necessarily her reflections on totalitarianism (see *The Ori-*

gins of Totalitarianism) or specifically on Eichmann but her insights into the "politics" of the person which is constitutive of *who* we are.³ Politics, she contends, is the essential space where we as human beings unfold our identity. Politics occupies a public space where we as human beings are made visible. It is integral to *who* we are and we cannot simply hide from this dimension of life. In other words, we cannot pull the shutters down on our identity. She sees the political realm as rising "directly out of acting together"; it consists of "that sharing of words and deeds." She says that the political dimension "is the space of appearance in the widest sense of the word . . . where I appear to others as others appear to me, where . . . [human beings] exist not merely like other living or inanimate things but make their appearance explicitly."[4]

A New Responsibility

After the burning of the Reichstag in 1933, Arendt said, "from that moment on I felt responsible. That is, I was no longer of the opinion that one can simply be a bystander." She was eventually arrested for collecting information on "anti-Semitic statements made in ordinary circumstances." After eight days of imprisonment, she was released and fled to France to work for Jewish refugee groups. In Gurs, southern France, she was imprisoned as an enemy alien. In 1941, she finally traveled to New York, where she lectured and held academic positions at several American universities, including Princeton, Berkeley, and Chicago. Arendt regarded herself primarily as a political theorist, seeing her writing as part of a process of understanding. She once remarked how "men always want to be terribly influential . . . [but] I want to understand. And if others understand . . . that gives me a sense of satisfaction, like feeling at home."[5]

Seeing through the Eyes of the "Other" Person

Arendt's theory of human action made an original contribution to twentieth-century political thought. We can see evidence of her unique analysis in the already mentioned study *Eichmann in Jerusalem*. In *The Human Condition*, she points out how what she proposes is really very simple. It is, she says, "*nothing more than to think what we are doing*."[6] But, of course, "not thinking" things through, perhaps one of the outstanding characteristics of our time, was evident in the case of Adolph Eichmann. The decisive flaw in his character was, she argues, a "total inability ever to look at anything from the other person's point of view."[7] Arendt characterizes this as radical "thoughtlessness," remarking, "There was no sign in him [Eichmann] of firm ideological convictions or of specific evil motives, and the only notable characteristic one could detect in his past behavior as well as in his behavior during the trial ... was something entirely negative: it was not stupidity but *thoughtlessness*."[8]

Unlike *a person* such as Edith Stein, Eichmann was completely unable to put himself into the place of the "other" person. He could never self-transcend, thereby placing himself in the shoes of the "other." In Arendt's perspective, Eichmann was not an "acting" person at all. He just "functioned." But Eichmann was not put on trial simply because he was a cog in a machine of hatred. In the last decade of her life, Arendt reflected further on the Eichmann in Jerusalem story. She observes how the judges "took great pains to point out explicitly, in a courtroom, *there is no system on trial ... no ism ... but a person. ...* [who] stands accused precisely *because even a functionary is still a human being*, and it is in this capacity that ... [a person] stands trial."[9]

Of course, Eichmann's shallowness was not unique, but he lived in an "upside-down world" of his own making. Arendt pointed out that Adolph Eichmann was not just the face of hatred and madness, but the personification of "the faceless nature of Nazi evil itself, within a closed system run by pathological gangsters" who aimed at destroying the "personhood" of its victims.[10] It was, of course, his "going-along-with-the-rest and wanting-to-say 'we'" that resulted in "the greatest of all crimes possible."[11] As a "functionary," he was "a very dangerous gentleman."[12] Eichmann was intelligent, but "it was his stupidity that was so outrageous." This is what she meant when she used the controversial term "banality" in the subtitle of her book, which caused so much controversy. There is nothing deep in Adolph Eichmann's "stupidity," there is "nothing demonic" in it. There is, she claimed, simply *the reluctance ever to imagine what the other person is experiencing*.[13]

Language as First Casualty

Arendt believed that Eichmann's case demonstrates how language defeated him. He used only slogans, saying at his trial, "Officialese is my only language." She explained how he was "genuinely incapable of uttering a single sentence that was not a cliché."[14] Arendt observed how the longer you listened to him, "the more obvious it became that his inability to speak was closely connected with an inability to *think*, namely, to think from the standpoint of someone else." Communication with him was impossible not because he lied but because he was surrounded "by the most reliable of all safeguards against the words and presence of others, and hence against reality as such."[15] Arendt argued how we too can be shielded "against reality and factuality" by the "same self-deception, lies and stupidity that had now become ingrained in Eichmann's mentality."[16] This is how his evil action was, in a sense, "banal" or "ordinary." In Fyodor Dostoevsky's *The Brothers Karamazov*, the devil appears to Ivan in the form of a mild-mannered, poor, elderly gentleman, not as a Frankenstein-like monster. So too for Arendt, when you encounter figures like Eichmann and even Hitler and Stalin, you witness their "personal mediocrity"; but then you witness the horrendous evil they unleash on the world. This is the shock and horror of it all as it emerges within the very "ordinariness" of their human natures. The Israeli court psychiatrist who examined Eichmann found him a "completely normal man, more normal at any rate, than I am examining him."

In her investigations, Hannah Arendt was ever aware of the need to come to terms with forms of human action that defy human understanding. She saw the German text of the taped police interrogation of Eichmann, "a veritable gold mine for a psychologist." Nonetheless, Arendt faced hostile reactions from different quarters for her analysis. Controversially, she wrote how "the horrible can be not only ludicrous but outright funny."[17] Indeed, as mentioned, her use of the term "banality" in terms of evil met with rancorous critique. Nevertheless, her analysis shed light on how evil, in fact, need not be committed by demonic monsters but by people like Eichmann. Its horror lies in its ordinariness stemming from a failure to "think," which is an indispensable characteristic of *who* we are as human persons. Arendt describes how "it was his [Eichmann's] absence of thinking" that awakened her interest as a political theorist in an investigation of the trial in Jerusalem.

Only Doing His Duty

During his prosecution, Eichmann declared that he had lived his whole life according to Immanuel Kant's moral principles, that is, doing his "duty" and being a law-abiding citizen. He declared that he had even read Kant's *Critique of Practical Reason*. During the trial, Eichmann gave his own version of what is called Kant's categorical imperative, that is, "the principle of my will must always be such that it can become the principle of general laws." Arendt comments that "this formulation was outrageous... and also incomprehensible, since Kant's moral philosophy is so closely bound up with" the human person's faculty of "judgment."[18] Eichmann, however, forgot the "inconvenient truth" that Dostoevsky and Kant highlighted, and which appears in *The Brothers Karamazov*: "above all else, never lie to yourself."[19] In *The Life of the Mind*, Arendt went on to examine three fundamental faculties of the *acting* human person: "thinking, willing and judging," which for Adolph Eichmann were reduced to "the will of the Führer."[20]

New Beginnings: "Natality"

In *The Human Condition*, Arendt reflects on what she calls "natality" as being central to human action. Disagreeing with Heidegger's famous dictum that we are beings "towards-death," she would say that we are beings "towards-birth." She observes how "the new beginning inherent in birth can make itself felt in the world because the newcomer possesses the capacity of beginning something anew."[21] She sees this idea of "initiative" as inherent in all human action and especially in political life. The fact of "natality" gives rise to the miracle of the "birth of new" persons and to new beginnings. As human beings, we can "begin again." We are capable of this virtue by reason of being born. Eichmann clearly lacked this unique human capacity. "Natality" is the miracle that saves us and the world from death. Arendt explains how it is in this human capacity for "new beginnings" that faith in and hope for the world can be found. Its "most glorious and succinct expression" is found in the few words with "which the Gospels announced their 'glad tidings': 'A child has been born unto us.'"[22]

Ten

Dietrich Bonhoeffer (1906–1945): Journey to the Center of the Person

Who Am I?

Dietrich Bonhoeffer was a Lutheran pastor, theologian, philosopher, writer, and martyr. In a poem written before his execution at Flossenbürg concentration camp, he asks "Who am I? This or the Other?" He explains how these questions constantly assail him. He ends up saying, "Who am I? They mock, they mock me, these lonely questions of mine. Whoever, I am, You know, O God, I am Yours."[1]

Notwithstanding the physical incarceration of the camp, Bonhoeffer understands that to answer the question "Who am I?" as a human person, I must escape the penitentiary of the "self." That is to say, I cannot fully appreciate myself as a human being if I stay trapped within my own world. In other words, I can only fully appreciate "*myself*" as "*another*." In a letter from 1944, Bonhoeffer notes how "if one has completely renounced making something of oneself... then one throws oneself into the arms of God." He holds that this "is faith; this is metanoia [conversion]. And this is *how one becomes a human being, a Christian*."[2] Indeed, the martyrs to National Socialism like Bonhoeffer, the young Jesuit Alfred Delp, and Edith Stein, show us how it takes only "a few extraordinary individuals to ward off phenomena of moral and spiritual decline in a given society" and recapture *who* we are as human beings.[3] Alfred Delp, for example, who we discuss in the next chapter, clearly saw the challenges. He saw the great task as being "in the education of present and

93

future generations" in restoring us "*to a state of fitness for God.*" The mission is "a desperate one of helping create conditions in *which man can return to himself, recover something of his lost humanity.*"[4] If Hannah Arendt spoke of the hope of "natality," Delp speaks of how the challenge is to "bring order to the chaos . . . and *then trust to the emergence of a new human being.*" He spoke of how a new approach is necessary involving education "*toward transcendence.*"[5] It is quite clear that none of these martyrs were guilty of the "sin of abstraction," since we see in their lives the collapse of the priority of the "theoretical" and a shift toward the "existential." Unfolding within each of them, as we hope to discover in this book, are crucial insights into what it means "*to be*" a person.

Creation and Fall

Dietrich Bonhoeffer lectured at the University of Berlin during the winter semester of 1932–33. His lectures, a theological reflection on the book of *Genesis* chapters one to three, were published subsequently with the apparently innocent but quite provocative title *Creation and Fall*.[6] This was, after all, a time of great confusion in Germany with the collapse of the Weimar Republic and the birth of the Third Reich. During this period, Bonhoeffer encourages his young students to "focus their attention on the word of God as the word of truth in a time of turmoil." Even within the history of Christianity during the second and early third centuries, there were the dangers of downplaying the Old Testament. This emerged once again during the times of the Third Reich and the rise of anti-Semitism. During Nazism, there was, in fact, a whole attempt to "de-Judaize" the Bible.[7] Consequently, Bonhoeffer's lectures were deliberate in tone and theme. Students flocked to listen to him, which did not go down well with the powers that be.

In *Creation and Fall*, Bonhoeffer focuses on the questions of *who* we are and our relationship with each other. He understands the human person as intrinsically social. God's identity is essentially communicated through the "You" of the "other." Bonhoeffer notes how we speak of the human being as the image of God. The "image," he says, is "relation." It is a relationship of a "You" to an "I." It is, he argues, an "analogy of relation." The "likeness" between God and humankind is "relationship." The "image that is like God" is "relationality," and this is *who* God is among us.[8] This is our fundamental calling as human beings. The experience of the Fall, of course, is always a reality that entails transgressing the boundaries of *who* we are and forgetting our role in God's creation. Bonhoeffer explains,

> The center has been intruded upon.... Now humankind stands in the middle, with no limit. Standing in the middle means living from its own resources [its own "I"] and no longer from the center. Having no limit means being alone. To be in the center and to be alone means to be sicut deus. Humankind is now sicut deus; it no longer needs the Creator.

Bonhoeffer explains to his students how this means that "Adam is no longer a creature. Adam has torn himself away from his creatureliness. Adam is sicut deus."[9] In the Hitlerian ideology this obviously leads to the creation of the new race of "supermen" or "new men" divorced from participation in a universal humanity. In all of this, we can decipher an ongoing transformation from human beings understood as created in *imago Dei* into *imago hominis*. Persons are thereby emptied of *who* they are and "dehumanized." Indeed, Eric Voegelin notes how the nutshell of the whole difficulty with Adolf Hitler was "*dedivinizing*," which leads to "*dehumanizing*." Voegelin explains that participation in the divine constitutes *who* we are as persons. We catch a glimpse of this insight in Bonhoeffer's words in the poem cited earlier: "Whoever, I am, You know, O God, I am Yours." Voegelin declares "dedivinizing is always followed by a dehumanizing. One cannot dedivinize oneself without dehumanizing oneself—with the consequences of dehumanization that we shall still have to deal with."[10]

Thus, for Dietrich Bonhoeffer the story of the Fall was not only about Adam and Eve but was now happening in Germany. But this is not only an occurrence of the past since any society can hurtle easily into a world of total "immanence" where there is the "nonexperience" of the "beyond" (the transcendent). Bonhoeffer devoted an entire lecture to "The Fall."[11] He points out how "this deed done by human beings who God created" is "a deed done by humanity." He says that "no human being can absolve himself from it." It is true that "Adam falls through Eve, and Eve through Adam." But this does not mean that the other person "relieves me of my burden; *instead I am infinitely burdened with the guilt of the other.*"[12]

Nonetheless, Bonhoeffer's thought is not despondent, since he highlights how despite the broken relationship, we are reconciled in Christ and recreated "into a new humanity."[13] As human persons we are, therefore, this "new creation" and "new humanity." Indeed, there is a similarity here with Alfred Delp's thoughts about "*the emergence of a new human being*" which we explore in the next chapter. Toward the end of Bonhoeffer's lectures on the first three chapters of Genesis, he speaks of Cain. He describes

> the end of Cain's history, and so the end of all history... is Christ on the cross, the murdered Son of God. That is the last desperate assault on the gate of paradise. And under the whirling sword, under the cross, the human race dies. But Christ lives. The trunk of the cross becomes the wood of life [zum Holze des

Lebens], and now in the midst of the world, on the accursed ground itself, life is raised up anew. In the center of the world, from the wood of the cross, the fountain of life springs up.... The tree of life, the cross of Christ, the center of God's world that is fallen but upheld and preserved, that is what the end of the story about paradise is for us.[14]

In Jesus Christ, Bonhoeffer says, "*God became human*," and thus, "human beings are set free to be truly human." He discloses how being a Christian "is not something beyond the human" but entails being "in the midst of the human." He reasons that to live as a human being before God means to live "not for oneself, but for God and other human beings."[15]

The Primacy of the "Other"

In light of this, we can speak of "Jesus' 'being-there-for-others,'" which in itself is the experience of transcendence. God makes himself one with us in Christ and restores us to our original "image" as human persons, that is, in *relationship* with God. Jesus lived out the primacy of the "other," and faith basically means "participating *in this being of Jesus*. In actually "being-there-for-others" we can re-establish our relationship to God in a new way. Bonhoeffer stresses how "the transcendent is not the infinite, unattainable task, but *the neighbor within reach in any given situation, God in human form!*" In this perspective God is not a concept but rather "the human being for others! therefore the Crucified One."[16] Of course, living this out in life costs; it does not come to us cheaply. Bonhoeffer remarks how "cheap grace means grace as bargain-basement goods" whereas "costly grace is the hidden treasure in the field ... the costly pearl."[17] Jesus on the cross paid the price of living the priority of the "other." God enters the world into our own time and lives with us every time we take the path of living for the "other" even unto it costing our lives. Bonhoeffer explained that being a Christian does not entail being religious in a particular way *"but to be a human being."* Indeed, this is *how* Bonhoeffer lived his life paying the costly price in his own life. He said before his execution "this is the end. For me the beginning of life." Following the series of lectures on Genesis, Bonhoeffer's authorization to teach at Berlin University was eventually revoked.

"Presence" in "Absence": Novel Ways of "Communion"

On Christmas Eve 1943, Dietrich Bonhoeffer wrote a letter, in many ways prophetic, to his close friends Renate and Eberhard Bethge. He speaks to them about the experiences of separation and absence involved in the death of someone. He writes,

> Nothing can replace the absence of someone dear to us, and one should not even attempt to do so; one must simply preserve and endure it. At first it sounds very hard, but at the same time is a great comfort, for one remains connected to the other person through the emptiness to the extent it truly remains unfilled. It is wrong to say that God fills the emptiness; God in no way fills it but rather keeps it empty and thus helps us preserve—even if in pain—our authentic communion.[18]

For Bonhoeffer, becoming truly human means acknowledging that we do not merely "invest the present [moment] with eternal value" or remain just focused upon ourselves. According to his viewpoint, true "presence" can also be experienced in apparent "absence," leading us to search for and live in new ways of genuine communion with one another. In a letter dated August 21, 1944, he remarks how we may think "that our own life has meaning because this or that other person exists." But, in fact, we have meaning only because "a human being like Jesus lived." Had he not lived "then our life would be meaningless, despite all other people we know, respect, and love."[19] And this is to respond to Bonhoeffer's question, "Who am I?" truthfully, knowing, as he says, that we are totally His.

Eleven

Alfred Delp, SJ (1907–1945): Epiphany of the Person

Nameless Persons

I never read much of Thomas Merton, but I have reflected on his "Introduction" to Alfred Delp's *Prison Writings*.[1] In many ways, it is just a reflection upon Delp's meditations, but it is often insightful to see and understand someone through the eyes of another. Some quotes from the "Introduction" are helpful. He writes:

> These pages are completely free from the myopic platitudes, and the insensitive complacencies of routine piety.... One of the most sobering aspects of this book is the conviction it imparts that *we may one day be in the same desperate situation as the writer*.... The meditations of Father Delp were written not only in the face of his own death, *but in the specter of a faceless being that was once the image of God* and toward which the Church nevertheless retains an unchanging responsibility.[2]

Merton's use of the word "specter" reminds me of the first words of Karl Marx and Friedrich Engels's *The Communist Manifesto* that "a spectre is haunting Europe—the spectre of communism."[3] A "specter" is a threat, and Marx and Engels do not actually see communism as a danger, and so they want to meet what they call "this nursery tale of the Spectre of Communism" with a clear articulation of their party manifesto. I mention Marx and Engels here deliberately. St. John Paul II said of Marx that his analysis of "alienation" was probably the best you can get, but his solution was anthropologically mistaken. Thus, Marx gave a penetrating analysis of the conditions of workers. Engels sent reports to Marx, who based himself in the British Library at the time. Engels's father, in fact, was a factory owner and proprietor in England. John Paul II notes how Marx got it wrong in terms of addressing or even asking the question, "who do you say that I am?" Indeed, Marx's *Economic and Philosophic Manuscripts of 1844* includes the phrase "*denke nicht und frage mich nicht*" ["don't think and don't ask me"] that can easily be applied to the question about *who* we are as human beings.[4] But as we shall see, Alfred Delp did not shy away from such difficult questions.

In my view, Delp's life can be understood not only as a tragic story but as a way in which we can uncover "the specter" of what a "faceless being" which was once "the image of God" entails for a society as a whole. In a small book, *Humanity and History,* Delp recalled how "the human being's responsibility is always to reflect the image of God." Within the shadowlands of Nazism and indeed many other "isms" there extended the deforestation of the "*humanscape*" into a terrain populated by persons *who*, in the eyes of those regimes, became nameless. Delp notes how "I myself don't count as a person anymore, but only as a number. Here in prison I'm number 1442, in cell 8/313."[5]

Spiritual and Anthropological Excavations

Phenomenology, an approach as we have seen in philosophy which focuses on human experience (and favored by Pope John Paul II), concludes that reality is not appearance. Since, in the words of Josef Pieper, appearance is "unreality,"[6] it is not the whole truth of the matter. There is a need to get to the "thing-in-itself." Or, we can say, to get to the "person-in-themselves." Delp's experiences stripped him of hanging onto mere appearances, opening a journey for him to the center of what it means to be a human person. Some of his letters give you a sense of this odyssey. After a severe beating at the hands of SS men, he is brought back to the prison late one evening. The SS guards leave him with the words: "You're not going to be able to sleep tonight. *You'll pray, but there will be no God, no angel to deliver you.* But we'll sleep and tomorrow morning we'll have our strength back to give you another thrashing."[7] In the chapter on Bonhoeffer, I spoke about the reality of "presence" in "absence." And this is somewhat similar to Delp's experience. In a letter to Luise Oestrreicher (November 1944), Delp explains how, after the beating, "During that night I saw that the whole fateful course of events was going to be as it later turned out. *God has encountered me.* Now it's up to me."[8]

Mary Frances Coady comments on Delp's realizing "how much of his pre-prison God-talk had been so much rhetoric, that his spiritual nakedness in the presence of God within the confines of his cell was of a new and terrifying order." We come across this kind of insight when we hear of Bonhoeffer praying, '*O God, why are you so terrifyingly close to us?*' Delp writes:

> And look at me now. Until now I did everything in a false manner... I'm only a beaten and failed human being. May the walk across the tightrope be taken in God's name...
>
> [T]he world is full of God: God comes even in misery and there is encounter, the need for discernment.... I'm aware that I am on a tightrope.... During the late evening I read from the seventh book of the *Republic*: Plato's famous cave image... from shadow to reality.... God is going to bring me across the tightrope.... It is strange how a person can live a double life, saying one thing, knowing another and feeling another.[9]

In December 1944, he describes how "God has become almost tangible. Things I have always known and believed now seem so concrete. I believe them, but I also live them."[10] Delp admits that up to his imprisonment, he lived a "Jekyll-and-Hyde" existence.[11] He confesses, "I also cheated my fellow human beings of many substantial blessings because I was incapable of taking really seriously God's command that we should trust him absolutely."[12]

"…All of Life Is Advent"

Delp did not keep a diary in prison, but he wrote many letters that were smuggled out. He was incarcerated during the Advent and Christmas season, and therefore many of the themes are about the coming of Jesus into our world. These meditations on Advent and Epiphany are highly recommended to the reader. Concerning the First Sunday of Advent, he observes:

> Unless we have been shocked to our depths at ourselves and the things we are capable of, as well as the failings of humanity as a whole, we cannot understand the full import of Advent. . . . *Life is both powerless and futile in so far as by itself it has neither purpose nor fulfilment. . . . It is necessary to be conscious of God's decision to enlarge the boundaries of his own supreme existence by condescending to share ours.* . . . It follows that life, fundamentally is a continuous Advent.[13]

Epiphany of the Person

In terms of the overall theme of *who* we are as human persons, Delp says "*God helps us find ourselves.*" He argues that if we forget this, we are living a lie. If we reject this insight, "We have committed an unpardonable *sin against our own being and the only way to correct it is through an existential reverse—back again to the truth."* This "return" must happen *now*.[14] Discussing the dangers of focusing on a language of "self-fulfillment," Delp reminds us that "unless a person reaches out ... the only alternative is to vegetate—and a person who vegetates ends by becoming less than human."[15]

Speaking about the Christmas feast, Delp says, "we ought to remember we are approaching the feast of God-made-man, not of man rendered divine." He declares that "in the darkest cells and the loneliest prisons we can meet him; he is continually on the high roads and in the lanes."[16] Within these reflections on Epiphany emerges the reality of what it means to be a human person. A human being is truly lost only when he or she is "incapable of a great inner sense of depth and freedom." Anyone who does not live life in "an atmosphere of freedom" is, according to Delp, "already lost." In fact, such a person "is not really a human being anymore; he is merely an object, a number."[17]

It can be that I "unbecome" *who* I am. We are free to be or not to be. Epiphany is a manifestation; it is a living out of *who* we are. Delp explains:

> We must leave ourselves behind if we hope to have even a glimpse of our potentialities.... Only when we trim our sails to the eternal winds do we begin to understand the sort of journey we are capable of undertaking.... *Human beings can become themselves only by stepping outside of themselves....* If in the midst of this frightfulness we can learn to pray, *then this hell will bring forth a new human being.*[18]

In his "Epiphany" reflections, Delp refers to the significance of "the wilderness" in the journey. The fact that the Lord retired into "the wilderness" shows how he took to heart the "problems of humanity." Delp describes how "the wilderness has a necessary function in life. 'Abandonment' as one of my friends called it and the word is very apt. . . . Abandonment to the silence of God, the greatest abandonment of all."[19]

"The Divine Comedy"

On February 2, 1945, Alfred Delp was executed in a Berlin prison. He said to the chaplain beforehand, "In half an hour . . . I'll know more than you do." Delp's life is a model of how the human person can go beyond the wounds of imperfection, even in the context of exterior confinement and excruciation. The spiritual writer Chiara Lubich's inspiring reflection, "The Divine Comedy," sums up how "negatives" can become "positives" (which was the case for Alfred Delp) if we embrace sufferings as Jesus did in his experience of forsakenness:

> Every time you feel despair in your soul,
> and you keep smiling and speaking of hope to the others;
> every time you feel death in your soul,
> and you keep smiling and speaking to the others of life;
> every time you feel in sin,
> and you keep smiling and speaking to the others of love, and love concretely,
> every time your soul is plunged into pitch darkness,
> and you keep smiling and speaking to others of light:
> you'll seem to be acting out a comedy,
> not to be living in the truth;
> then remember: that is the divine comedy,
> that is the pure ideal,
> that is *to be* Jesus Forsaken.[20]

Twelve

Emmanuel Levinas (1901–1995): A Spirituality of "Proximity"

Beyond "Being"

Emmanuel Levinas, a French Jewish philosopher, was born in Kaunas, Lithuania. He studied philosophy in Strasbourg, France. In 1940, he was captured by the Nazis and imprisoned in a labor camp for officers. His Lithuanian family were all murdered, but his wife and daughters were hidden by religious nuns in Orléans. From 1947 onward, he took up various academic positions in France. Speaking about Martin Buber and Emmanuel Levinas, St. John Paul II noted how their writings approximate very closely to the thought of Thomas Aquinas. But in these philosophers, he suggests, the pathway to understanding reality and ourselves passes not through careful considerations of "being" and "existence" but through people and their meeting each other. It is through the "I" and the "Thou" of each other as human beings that we comprehend the "Other."[1] In a way, Levinas's whole philosophical approach can be understood from the perspective we set out in *Myself as Another*. Levinas affirms that it is "my inescapable and incontrovertible answerability to the other that makes me an individual 'I.'"[2]

New Horizons on Transcendence

Levinas also inaugurated a new approach in arriving at the "transcendent," an innovative direction in philosophy. Indeed, David Walsh suggests how through Levinas's contribution, "modern philosophy, which began with the centering of attention on the self, has now recognized that its very project is constituted by what lies beyond it."[3] The search for the "beyond" is usually "mediated through the sacred," but for Levinas, it is in the "face" of the "other" that we encounter and directly experience the "beyond." To Levinas, this is not an abstract reality since that would be an "untrue" transcendence. The "other" "demands me, requires me, summons me."[4] Levinas explains how "the face-to-face is a relation in which the *I* frees itself from being limited to itself." In the encounter with the "other" person, we experience an "exodus from that limitation of the *I* to itself."[5]

Of course, as we have seen, many other philosophers like Søren Kierkegaard, Martin Buber, and Gabriel Marcel reflected on what is often called a philosophy of the "Other." The challenge, according to Levinas, is not to get caught up in a tangle of abstractions. In loving one's neighbor and "working on oneself," we can "go toward the Other where he is truly other." Levinas understands love as "a movement by which a being seeks that to which it was bound before even taking the initiative."[6] It may seem that "love" heads "toward immanence, but it is defined by transcendence."[7] Levinas calls this emphasis on "the presence" and "proximity of persons" a "new spirituality."[8]

Levinas observes that addressing another person causes an "ethical disturbance" within us. We cannot remain indifferent to them. It is as if "the tranquility of the perseverance of my being, in my egoism" is shattered in the encounter. Accordingly, when I meet a stranger, I am provoked to go outside of myself and it is then that "all thought is subordinated to the *ethical relation*, to the infinitely other in the other person."[9] As a result, Levinas holds that "love" is not just consciousness of the "other." Any thinking (*cogito*) about the "other" follows on from our preexisting "vigilance for the other." Whereas Descartes emphasized the *cogito* in the famous dictum "I think, therefore, I am," Levinas focuses on the priority of the "other." Putting it in philosophical terms, he says, "the transcendental *I* in its nakedness comes from *the awakening by and for the other*."[10]

The Proximity of the "Other"

Levinas highlights what he calls "the proximity of the other," seeing it as putting into question our very "being" as human persons. He speaks of how we can, of course, live purely at the level of "there is" (*il y a*). The concept of "there is," as in statements like "it is raining [*il pleut*]" or "it's a nice day" [*il fait beau*], remains at the "absolutely-impersonal" level. But when we come to human beings, we move beyond the mere "recognition of things [*choses*]." In this experience, the human subject realizes that it cannot be "sufficient unto itself." Levinas describes how it is in "that I-You relation" that we are "immediately in society." "We are," he says, "in a society in which we are equal in relation to one another." Levinas asserts "I am to the other what the other is to me."[11] Thus, I am myself as another.

It is the meeting with the "other" which facilitates "the first exiting from self."[12] In experiencing the "other" I can, so to speak, let go of myself. The "other" human person is, therefore, the threshold to transcendence. In the encounter with them, I can pass through to the "Other." The "Other" is in our midst and is as proximate to us as in the neighbor. The epiphany of the human face, in the Levinasian perspective, actually "constitutes a penetration of the crust" of the human being who is "preoccupied with itself." Levinas speaks of how our responsibility before the "other" turns out to be "the 'disinterested' for-the-other of saintliness." This type of vocation of holiness, according to Levinas, is what essentially defines the human. He is not saying that human beings are "saints." Levinas means that the acknowledgment of the importance of responsibility for the "other" is, in fact, a recognition that defines what it is to be a human being. In this way, the human has pierced through "the imperturbable being; even if no social organization, nor any institution can . . . ensure, or even produce saintliness."[13]

Priority of the "Other": "Saintliness"

In a 1987 interview, Levinas explains how "the encounter with the other is the great event" and this cannot be reduced to the mere acquisition of knowledge. It might be the case that I can never totally understand the other but "the responsibility for him, where language is born and the social instinct with it, overflows knowing" as such.[14] In answer to the question, "what is ethics?" he answers, "it is the recognition of 'saintliness.'" He outlines how the fundamental preoccupation of each individual being is its own being. When it comes to the world of plants and animals "all living things hang onto their lives." In each case, it is all about "the struggle for survival." But when you come to the encounter with the human you have the *"possible advent of an ontological absurdity."* The experience, he says, is that "the concern for the other is greater than the concern for oneself. This is what I call 'saintliness.' *Our humanity consists in being able to recognize the priority of the other.*"[15]

Levinas is asked, "can this attention to others be taught?" He replies that it is awakened before the "face" of the other and believes that in putting the other person first "God comes to mind." Human existence lived in terms of this priority of the other is transcendence. It means we "escape" or *ex-it* ourselves. There is, Levinas says, a deep need "to come out of being" and not remain "cramped inside a tight suffocating circle."[16] He holds that when he uses the term "face" he means the "other." Indeed, when we think of the experiences during the international pandemic, when we all had to wear masks, we can easily understand what Levinas has in mind. The "face" is what is behind the mask; because it is "behind the façade and under the countenance that each person gives himself."[17] Indeed, the challenge was that we could not even see each other face-to-face, which ends up deconstructing *who* we are as human persons. Levinas is asked: *Is the other of whom you speak also the altogether-Other of God?* His answer is interesting. He says the "Other of God" is there "in that priority of the other" person over me. It is there well before "my admiration for the creation, well before my research of the first cause of the universe." He explains how "theology begins for me in the face of one's fellow man.... God descends in the face of the other."[18]

The Wisdom of Love

When asked, "what is philosophy?" Levinas explains that traditionally it is understood as the "love of wisdom," but he sees it as the "wisdom of love." At times we can run the risk of being intoxicated solely by "the rhythm of words and the generalities they express." Consequently, there is a continual need and challenge to "be awakened" by the "other." In this way, we can open ourselves up to "the uniqueness of the unique in the real" in which we discover the distinctiveness of other persons. Levinas calls philosophy a kind of "insomnia," that is, it keeps us, or should do so, continually awake to *who* the "other" really is. He describes how "transcendence is what faces us [in the 'other']. A face breaks up the system." In masking up during the health crisis, we missed the experience of a "face which looks at me affirming me." It is when we are "face to face" that we can "no longer negate the other." He says we cannot "escape the face of the neighbor."[19] Levinas describes how "the biological brotherhood—conceived with the sober coldness of Cain—is not sufficient reason for me to be responsible" for another. Cain's coldness consists in understanding responsibility only in terms "of a contract." But responsibility in front of the neighbor is not based on this. Before the neighbor, the "stony core of my substance is dislodged." The encounter with the "other" calls "upon my responsibility" and "forbids me any replacement." I am "unreplaceable in responsibility."[20] Our awakening to this reality can be described as a "shudder of the incarnation through which *giving* takes on meaning . . . in which a subject becomes a heart." In a Levinasian perspective, it is in living out this priority that we become and discover *who* we are as human beings.[21]

Thirteen

Simone Weil (1909–1943): "Gravity" and "Grace" of *Who* We Are

Living like Caged Birds

Simone Weil was born in Paris to Jewish parents. She entered the *École Normale Supérieure*, University of Paris, in 1928. Afterward, she taught for some time in various high schools throughout France. She also tutored workers in factories and field laborers in philosophy. In Southern France, during wine harvest times, she recalls carrying a copy of Plato's *Symposium*, eagerly sharing, and explaining it to others. Because she was always interested in the first-person perspective in terms of human experience, in 1934 she spent a sabbatical year working in Parisian car factories like those of Alstom and Renault. This was a major turning point for her, both philosophically and religiously. She directly experienced what she called the humiliation and dehumanization of industrialization while working on the factory floor. In her journals and writings, she clearly records these harsh experiences and recalls the continuous and repetitive orders from bosses and the inhuman pressure to keep pace with the mechanized production process. The result was, according to Weil, fatigue ending up in no longer being able to think. And, of all things, Weil could not but think.

Tearing Our Souls to Shreds

Weil describes how this whole process ensnares workers into a kind of slavery, who become trapped like squirrels in a cage. In this situation, persons are no longer able to have thoughts, invent, or even exercise judgment. In short, you enter the shock of becoming a "thing," and this "contradiction lodged within the soul tears it to shreds."[1] Using Homer's *Iliad*, she tries to understand history and different phenomena like Hitlerism. The central theme of the *Iliad*, according to her, is "force." And "force" is that which turns anybody subjected to it "into a thing." It turns the human person "into a stone." In this context, the person becomes a "corpse before anybody or anything touches him."[2] She experienced this whole reality of alienation, as we have said, while working in factories. She witnessed how "this heavy emptiness" caused deep human suffering.[3] Nonetheless, we must face the reality, she says, that work includes an irreducible "element of servitude" that even a perfect society can never remove. Karl Marx spoke of "religion" as the "opium of the people" entrapping us.

But Simone Weil says that this applies more aptly to the idea of "revolution." She argues that "the hope of revolution is always a drug."[4] A change in external working or living conditions will not necessarily alter *who* we are as human persons. In *Person and Act*, St. John Paul II makes a similar point when he discusses alienation. Marx's view, he says, is that the person is alienated by "his products: economic and political systems, property and work." But this leads to the problematic conclusion that alienation will cease once you transform the structures.[5] The great falsehood at the heart of any adequate analysis of alienation, according to Weil, is to think that our souls can fly away from "the use to be made of disgust for work." Reflecting on "The Mysticism of Work," she describes how our greatness as human beings is our ability to recreate life, to recreate what is given to us, and to fashion our experience. It is through work that the human person "produces" their own existence. She believes that "disgust [experienced in work] in all its forms is one of the most precious trials sent to man *as a ladder by which to* rise.... Monotony is the most beautiful or the most atrocious of things. The most beautiful if it is a reflection of eternity—the most atrocious if it is a sign of an unvarying perpetuity. *It is time surpassed or time sterilized.*"[6] In fact, as human beings, we can recreate ourselves through work and should not run away from this opportunity. Through work, she writes, "time" enters "the body" and so is transformed.

Only Beauty Can Save Us

We remain as slaves, Weil says, if we simply continue "turning round and round" in circles, living lives out of mere "necessity."[7] This is to stay at the "vegetative level" of life. The slave is the one "to whom no good is proposed as the object of" their labor "except mere existence." So "to strive from necessity and not for some good" maintaining our existence just as it is, "that is always slavery." Weil suggests:

> *The beautiful alone enables us to be satisfied by that which is.* Workers need poetry more than bread. They need that their life should be a poem. They need some light from eternity. Religion alone can be the source of such poetry.... Slavery is work without any light from eternity, without poetry, without religion. May the eternal light give not a reason for living and working, but a sense of completeness which makes the search for any such reason unnecessary.[8]

The worst outrage for Weil is not necessarily physical deprivations but "the crime against" what she called the "*attention* of the workers." This word "attention" is of special significance to her. She held that only by the "supernatural working of grace can a soul pass through its annihilation to *the place where alone it can get the sort of attention which can attend to truth.*"[9] She declares that human beings are "unequal in all their relations with the things of the world." The truth, in fact, is that the only thing that we all share "*is the presence of a link with the reality outside the world.*" Only by "really directing the attention beyond the world" can we remain in real contact with this central "and essential fact of human nature."[10] Throughout her writings, she continually argues against people being considered just cogs in a machine, pointing out how such an approach "empties the soul of everything unconcerned with speed." As human beings, we are much more than gearwheels in a system, and we must *attend* to this reality.

Detachment

Weil believes that any exit strategy from oppression or alienation cannot be based upon revolutionary or utopic solutions. As we have seen, the Marxian analysis held that by changing the external economic and social structures, alienation is totally eradicated. But Weil's unique approach is unfolded in her philosophical reflections, where she considers how philosophy is not about the transfer or acquisition of different forms of knowledge. Reflection, she argues, is about the "transformation of the orientation of the soul, which we call *detachment*." Real change happens *within,* and this begins in *detachment*. In her essay "Philosophy" (1941), she points out that Plato originally outlined this particular "*way of living*." Referencing Plato's *Republic* (VI 518b–d), Weil stresses that "philosophy is to turn one towards the truth with all one's soul."[11] Plato says that the "art that is needed here is *the art of conversion*, which shows the easiest and the most effective way of making the soul turn." In her writings, she mentions several philosophical texts and sources originating from the Greeks, the *Bhagavata-Gita*, the Egyptians, Chinese, and European philosophers like Descartes and Kant that follow this tradition of *detachment*. These thinkers are interested in knowledge not for its own sake but because they are "orientated towards salvation."[12] To make a continual thoroughgoing investigation of human experience, we cannot remain "attached" to it but must "unfasten" from it. This demands an effort and to achieve it, she says, looks "like a miracle. The word 'grace' expresses this miraculous character."[13] Detachment is "a renunciation of all possible ends without exception" so that the soul can be orientated toward the truth of the "beyond."[14]

Weil suggests detachment not as an abstract concept, but as a way of life that applies equally to the encounter with what she calls "the work of human hands," which, as she observes, always contains suffering. She looks upon attachment as a "manufacturer of illusions and *whoever wants reality ought to be detached*." As we have said, speaking from her own personal experiences, Weil held that "experience proves that this waiting [to reach the moment of "grace," or insight] is satisfied. It is then we touch the absolute good."[15]

Christ "Emptied Himself"

In *Waiting for God*, Weil argues that on God's part "creation is not an act of self-expansion but of restraint and renunciation." She describes how God accepted "diminution." He "emptied part of his being from himself."[16] To Simone Weil, Christ was the model of a way of life of detachment. She observes:

> "He emptied himself of his divinity." To empty ourselves of the world. To take the form of a slave. To reduce ourselves to the point we occupy in space and time — that is to say, to nothing.
> To strip ourselves of the imaginary royalty of the world....
> Then we possess the truth of the world.[17]

In many ways, Weil anticipates some of St. John Paul II's thoughts in his encyclical on human work, *Laborem Exer-*

cens, where he speaks of "elements for a spirituality of work." He outlines how all work is linked with toil. In enduring the drudgery "of work in union with Christ crucified for us, man in a way collaborates with the Son of God for the redemption of humanity."[18] Through work we can enter the process of becoming *who* we are as persons. St. John Paul II says that in "the most ordinary of everyday activities" we unfold this reality.[19] Likewise, Simone Weil explained:

> Through work man turns himself into matter, as Christ does in the Eucharist. Work is like a death. We have to pass through death.... When the universe is weighing upon the back of a human creature, what is there to be surprised at if it hurts? ...
>
> To work—if we are worn out it means that we are becoming submissive to time as matter is. Thought is forced to pass from one instant to the next without laying hold of the past or the future.[20]

In her philosophical perspective, taking in the gravity and grace of who we are as human beings allows us to "turn around." It is interesting to note that Jacques Derrida often gave a copy of *Gravity and Grace* as a present to friends. I suppose he too might have reckoned that human life is marked by "gravity," and it is only "by receiving God's gift—grace—that we can be redeemed and life's questions, which are beyond our understanding, can be answered."[21]

Fourteen

Paul Ricoeur (1913–2005): Oneself as Another

A Life

The French philosopher Paul Ricoeur was born in Valence, Drôme, to a devout family of Huguenots (a French Protestant minority who suffered persecution during the sixteenth and seventeenth centuries). His mother died shortly after his birth and his father was killed at the start of World War I, leaving him an orphan, to be raised by his grandparents. A very devoted student, he read the great classics and went on to study philosophy at the University of Rennes, although his failure "to pass the entrance examination to the *École Normale Supérieure* marked" him for a long time.[1] The Second World War caught him by surprise "at the end of a beautiful summer spent" with his wife "at the University of Munich attending a German language class."

He ended up being drafted, became an officer, and was taken prisoner for five years.[2] During his captivity he read the works of Karl Jaspers. Ricoeur explains how he and his fellow POWs knew nothing of the horrors of the concentration camps until their liberation in the spring of 1945. At the end of the war, Ricoeur joyfully returned to his family and taught philosophy at high school for some time while doing his own writing and research. Before the war he had met Gabriel Marcel in Paris and was greatly influenced by him, saying that what he learned from Marcel was "always to supply examples. If you want to talk about justice, ask yourself why something is unjust."[3] After an appointment to teach at the University of Strasbourg, he went on to lecture at the Sorbonne. He also served as dean at the University of Paris, but these were difficult years for him because of the student riots of 1968. He lectured widely in the United States and Canada, teaching for some years at the University of Chicago. With Emmanuel Levinas and Leszek Kołakowski, he participated in the summer philosophy roundtables organized by Pope John Paul II at Castel Gandolfo, Rome. Interestingly, President Emmanuel Macron of France was an editorial assistant to Ricoeur for some time while he was a student.[4]

The Human Person: Capacities

When it comes to understanding *who* we are as human persons, Ricoeur places great emphasis "on the notion of *capacity*." There is danger in seeing humans only in terms of their "performance." Indeed, in the world of education and business, we might be familiar with the term "KPIs," that is, "key performance indicators" used in Quality Assurance projects. Ricoeur comments that "our society, still, is one in which we measure people on their performances, and not their capacities. Some of which have been stifled by society, by life, by illness." His approach is to find what he calls "the *capable human being* behind the *ineffective human being*, behind the *powerless human being*."

Ricoeur emphasizes how "it is in the capacity to be Human that the character of being deserving of respect lies." An interviewer once mentioned to Ricoeur how in French children's class books "*disabilities are almost never taken into account, or even mentioned, as if they were some sort of taboo.*" Ricoeur agreed: "Yes. It is true that we don't see the lame or blind in children's books." He remarked that Victor Hugo's famous novel *The Hunchback of Notre Dame* has sympathetic characters like Quasimodo the hunchback.

Nonetheless, Ricoeur points out that in children's books you will not often find those "with physical or mental disabilities ... because they frighten [away] children." He tells of the thalidomide scandal that broke out when he was in Canada. A friend of his at the University of Montreal oversaw the development of orthopedic equipment for children who had no arms. The children could learn to use their feet to write, but the teachers rejected this because "it was too distant from the human form."[5] Ricoeur points out how such a view supposes that "if there is no resemblance to the human form, it is unacceptable to children." Although it would have been simpler for the children to use *the capacity of their feet to write,* incredibly complicated devices were used. As we have already noted, Ricoeur places so much emphasis on the notion of *capacity* because it *"is in the capacity to be Human that the character of being deserving of respect resides."*[6] In his mind, the notion of the "capable has become absolutely central." It allows him to link an adequate anthropology, that is, "a general description of what it is to be a human being," with a morality that spells out how a person is worthy of respect because of "the capacity to be himself or herself."[7]

Our Fragility

Indeed, the main theme of Ricoeur's work *Oneself as Another* is "the acting suffering human being" who is, he holds, notwithstanding all, "the capable human being."[8] The human person, of course, is a being "capable of speaking, capable of acting, capable of promising."[9] But the human person is much more than this. The first maxim of my action is that "any other life, by reason of its capacities, is just as important as mine."[10] Ricoeur gives an account not just of our capabilities as human beings but also of our weaknesses and fragility. He once wrote to psychiatrist friends a short reflection titled *"La souffrance n'est pas la douleur"* [Suffering is not pain] outlining how suffering reaches us as human beings "in the entire panoply" of our capacities, that is, in our *"power to be* and not only" in our *power to do.*[11] For example, in their patients, psychoanalysts may encounter the "incapacity" to tell their story because they may be "overwhelmed by memories that are unbearable, incomprehensible, or traumatic."[12] Such an *incapacitation*, Ricoeur says, "is organic." But he says there are "so many levels of suffering" for human beings.[13] The recognition of this "incapacity" to communicate their story is, in fact, a "capacity" opening what it means to be a human person. Part of the paradox of *who* we are "over and against" the affirmation of our capabilities is the "confession of our fragility." In his analysis of "The Paradoxes of Identity," Ricoeur explains how "the inability-to-say, in all its forms . . . is the first mark of fragility."[14] Illness, old age, and disabilities are all instances of such fragility, but they do not unmake us as human persons. Ricoeur speaks of the condition of the "wounded *cogito,"* the realization that we are not, in fact, masters of ourselves. He describes how in today's world we are "under the threat of a claim, an appeal not to suffer, an appeal not to be sick, and even the formulation of a right to health." He sees this as leading to the idea that medicine is required "to shelter me from suffering."[15] According to Ricoeur, there is not necessarily a contradiction between "happiness" and "suffering." "Happiness" he understands as "the capacity to find meaning, satisfaction, in self-accomplishment," but this does not exclude "suffering." By suffering he does not simply mean pain. It is, he believes, "the reduction, even destruction of the capacity for acting, or being able to act."

Giving until the Very End

At a medical conference in Paris, Ricoeur referred to the human action involved in the palliative care of patients by medical staff. He recalled the words of the Danish philosopher, Peter Kemp: "What remains human, the last glimmer of the human, is the capacity to enter into relation 'giving and receiving.'" Ricoeur stresses how it is important to live in the reality of "giving and receiving... [even] when one can no longer do anything." We must, he says, defend this "capacity of exchange in *giving and receiving*" in the seriously ill patient to the very end. At the Paris conference, Ricoeur reflects on what medical staff receive in the gaze of their patients. It is, he argues, the *apprenticeship "of your own humanity."*[16]

Blessed Chiara Badano, a young Italian girl who died at the age of eighteen of bone cancer, is an example of someone going beyond the "wound," the pain of her condition. In a letter, she wrote how "now nothing healthy is left in me, but I still have my heart and with that I can still love." She was equally able to live "receiving." She wrote "I don't really do anything at all! On the contrary, it's all of you who are a help for me."[17] She, I believe, is an example of living out what Ricoeur calls the "capacity" and "fragility" of *who* we are as human beings. I recall what St. Paul wrote to the Christians at Corinth: "I am content with weaknesses, insults, hardships, persecutions... for when I am weak, then I am strong" (2 Cor 12:10). When someone told Chiara that she was deluded in her belief she replied: "*I have never seen God either, but I see him in you!*"[18]

Supplying an Example

I conclude this chapter on Paul Ricoeur by sharing a particular experience. He did remark, after all, that Gabriel Marcel reminded him to "always supply examples." The following experience unfolds a little, I believe, of what Ricoeur understood to be the "capable" and "fragile" nature of being human beings. For many years I was head chaplain at

University College Dublin, Ireland. Many Irish students go to the United States during the summer months on their J1 visas. They get jobs and experience a different culture. Employers seem to like Irish students since they are young, intelligent, and very friendly. Some of our students traveled to Berkeley, California. There for us as a nation a tragedy unfolded. A balcony collapsed; seven of our students died and many were very seriously injured. As a university chaplain, I immediately boarded an Aer Lingus flight to California along with the bereaved parents. It is a very long flight! I could tell you much more about this experience of suffering for the students and parents but let me just focus on one experience:

> I remember one day going around the hospitals in the aftermath and visiting the injured. I was in a hospital room with one of the families and a student. A nurse (Kim) came in to care for this severely injured student. After a while in the room, she asked if she could share an experience with us. She explained how she had suffered in her own life and how along the way some people were not very helpful to her. She ended up feeling treated like an object. But then she turned to the student and said *"Look, I see in you a very positive attitude, a real determination to live this awful event well. Believe it or not, you'll grow on the inside in all of this, you'll grow as a human person, you'll grow on the inside as a person."*

> Some days later I came back to visit the same student. I saw the same nurse in the reception area, and I shared with her how I'd found her words so moving. I explained that I often give lectures to students on Greek tragedy and how central was the idea of *pathei mathos*, that is, "wisdom comes through suffering." She

laughed at me [quite rightly!] and said *"well, whatever you call it in whatever language, it is true!"*

What the nurse said was very moving for us all. And indeed, even amid almost impossible odds, in all the students and families I witnessed and experienced the amazing capacity of their "self-determination." I will never forget the funeral vigil at St. Columba's Church in Oakland, California, where the families and the bodies of their loved ones were all reunited. I remember quite clearly that evening how some of the students who were severely injured had to remain in hospital. But their friends who could come to the funeral vigil used their iPhones so that those who were not there could "FaceTime" with their friends who died (to say a last goodbye). It brought tears to our eyes and broke our hearts. Yet there was a reality being lived, that is, that the love lived between us as human persons does not end in the moment of death. On the contrary, it can now be lived in a new way!

There are many other heroic stories of the capacity of these students in being determined to live for each other, of trying to break the fall of the other. They were and are witnesses to me of the powerful capacity Ricoeur speaks about for human beings to live for each other even in the context of great suffering. They and Chiara Badano are existential paradigms of living "oneself" as "another."

Fifteen

Etty Hillesum (1914–1943): The Girl who Learned to Kneel

Life Lived

Etty Hillesum's diaries and letters, written in the most extreme of personal circumstances, reveal an extraordinary portrait of the challenging reality of what it means to be a "person." In them, we discover someone who was "achingly conscious of what it meant to be a human person while experiencing that experience's polar opposite."[1] She honestly discloses in her diary entries, how she is constantly in "turmoil and commotion inside."[2] Her own family background was evidently Jewish although the Hillesums did not seem outwardly to practice their faith. But there are repeated allusions in the diaries to the likening of their journey and that of others to the wandering of the people of Israel in the desert. Etty clearly understands that the time for armchair theorizing is over.

She says, "they are out to *destroy us* [the Jewish people] completely."[3] Her own personal life, initially, bordered on the dysfunctional, and her family story was equally tragic, with her two brothers suffering from mental illness and experiencing many hospitalizations. She had a most difficult relationship with her parents. About her mother, she wrote, "Stop whining for goodness' sake, you shrew, you nag." She described how her "mother is someone who would try the patience of a saint." She tries to like her but says, "what a ridiculous and silly person" she was.[4] Hillesum tells how her parents "smother you, and nothing important ever happens. I would degenerate into a melancholic if I were to stay here for any length of time...I don't know what kind of madhouse this really is, but I know that no human being can flourish here."[5]

Journal of a Soul

The German Jungian psychotherapist Julius Spier recommended that she keep a journal. Indeed, throughout her diaries you can clearly see how much Spier influenced her. However, his own physical relationship with clients and students, like Hillesum, is regarded unquestionably as professional misconduct. The diaries are not just an investigative account of her trying to pinpoint her problems; they are also a therapeutic way in which she sought to regain *who* she was as a human being. She remarks how the worst thing for her will be when she is no longer allowed to have pencil and paper as she is finally transported to Auschwitz. These are, she says, "indispensable to me, for without them I shall fall apart and be utterly destroyed."[6] Reflecting on the work of the sculptor Auguste Rodin, she understands how it is only by means of an inner sculpting that she can give rebirth to *who* she is as a human person.[7]

Her diary narrative certainly records her harrowing experiences, but this is not all. She also "remakes" herself through the "inner articulation of the artistic process." She observes how "everything is a growing process," and this is the case too in becoming *who* we are. In her perspective, "nothing is pure chance." She speaks of how "if you have a rich inner life," then there is not much difference between the inside and the outside of the concentration camp. She admits in her diary that "life is going to be very hard. We shall be torn apart, all who are dear to one another...We shall have to steal ourselves inwardly more and more."[8]

This human capacity for creation of self by self happens continually in our lives.[9] The philosopher Henri Bergson notes how "this creation of self by self is the more complete, the more one reasons on what one does." He says that "for a conscious being, to exist is to change, to change is to mature, to mature is to go on creating oneself endlessly."[10] Writing is one way of doing this. We have only to think of the great writers like Aleksandr Solzhenitsyn who wrote novels like *One Day in the Life of Ivan Denisovich* and *The Gulag Archipelago*. In the *Gulag*, Solzhenitsyn would say, "*Bless you, prison*, for having been my life!"[11] The act of diaristic writing, if you like, presses the pause button in human experience, allowing Hillesum to actually defeat time. She conquers the awful events by "living" the present moment intensely. She says, "I know how to free my creative powers more and more from the snare of material concerns."[12]

Her writing results in the ripening of experiences, giving her the ability to recapture *who* she is, each entry of the diary becoming in itself a "creative act." She tells how "here on these pages I am spinning my thread. And a thread does run through my life, through my reality, like a continuous line."[13] She discovers that her life is "part" of a greater "whole." Whatever circumstances we find ourselves in, it is "possible to create, even without ever writing a word or painting a picture, by simply molding one's inner life."[14] Words are important for her since she sees each one as being like "a small milestone, a slight rise in the ground." But at the same time, the background to each human story is "wordless" because it is in "wordlessness" that "more happens than in all the words one can string together." In a diary entry for May 18, 1942, made after a visit to an art exhibition on Japanese prints at a nearby art gallery, she comments, "that's how I want to write…A few delicate brushstrokes…The great things that matter in life can be said in a few words…I would like to brush in a few words against a wordless background."[15]

No Enemies, No Hatred

An important insight Etty Hillesum reaches while she and her family are in Westerbork camp, Netherlands, awaiting transportation to Auschwitz, is that rottenness lies within each one of us. Her friend, Jan Bool, asked her, "what is it in human beings that makes them want to destroy each other?" She reproaches him, reminding him "that you're one [a human being] yourself." She sees how the only solution is "to turn inward and to root out all the rottenness there. I no longer believe that we can change anything in the world until we have first changed ourselves."

Jan agrees, saying "yes, it is too easy to turn your hatred loose on the outside, to live for nothing but the moment of revenge. We must try to do without that."[16] The eradication needed is "the evil in man, not man himself."[17] As we have previously noted, this is somewhat like Solzhenitsyn's remark in *The Gulag Archipelago*: "Gradually it was disclosed to me that the line separating good and evil passes not through states, nor between classes, nor between political parties either—*but right through every human heart—and through all human hearts.*"[18] Nonetheless, Hillesum says that many people remain hieroglyphs to her, but gradually she is learning to decipher them.

Like Solzhenitsyn, she explains that in Westerbork she experienced "life's innermost framework, stripped of all outer trappings." She adds, "thank You, God, for teaching me to read better and better."[19] She tells a friend, Klaas Smelik, "we have so much work to do on ourselves that we shouldn't be thinking of hating our so-called enemies."[20] The demarcation point concerning good and evil lies in our own hearts. She discovers how "Each of us must turn inward and destroy in himself all that he thinks he ought to destroy in others. And remember that every atom of hate we add to this world makes it still more inhospitable."[21] She jokes to Klaas Smelik how he will say to her, "but that—that is nothing but Christianity!" Her reply is, "Yes, Christianity, and why ever not?"[22]

In *Letters from Westerbork,* she gives an eyewitness account to her friends of the unfolding human catastrophe. She observes how it is even possible to live in "a prison within a prison." She argues that you need "a great deal of inner sunshine if you don't want to become the psychological victim of it all." She declares how "the barbed wire is more a question of attitude."[23] Looking reality straight in the face, the fact is, that every human being carries "deep in his inner being the trend, the part of society" which is playing out.[24] This is, in Plato's terms, the reality that "society" is simply the human person "written large," and to change it, we must begin with ourselves.[25]

Unbelievably, given the appalling circumstances, Hillesum remains positive about human nature, observing how we have the capacities and faculties to change and become *who* we are as human beings. She points out, "what distinguished each one of us was our inner attitudes."[26] Notwithstanding the horror experienced, human beings possess "inner freedom and independence," which no one can take away from them.[27] As persons, we are strong enough to move beyond the wound of multiple deprivations. She advises that we should give to sorrow all the space and shelter that is its due, but when you have given it its right place "then you can truly say: life is beautiful and so rich. So beautiful and so rich that it makes you want to believe in God."[28] Elsewhere in her *Diaries,* in almost a Julian of Norwich vein, she says, "have confidence that it will all come together and everything will turn out right in the end."[29] She holds that all human disasters stem from us, and we can overcome them by unshackling the love that is inside us "and giving it a chance to live."[30] As human beings, we have these unique capacities, and nothing or no one can take them from us. The greatest injury is the one we inflict on ourselves. The only solution is to transform "our hatred for our fellow human beings of whatever race...into love."[31] Etty Hillesum has no enemies, nor hatred; she declares: "I hate nobody. I am not embittered. And once the love of mankind has germinated in you, it will grow without measure."[32]

The Girl Who Learned to Kneel

Hillesum uses the image of how a spider spins a web by casting its web ahead of itself and then follows along. She tells how "the main path of my life stretches like a long journey before me and already reaches into another world."[33] In Westerbork, she recognizes that "you cannot play the ostrich" as a human person.[34] Commenting on her own life, she summarizes it by saying, "what a strange story it really is, my story: *the girl who could not kneel. Or its variation: the girl who learned to pray.*"[35] In a diary entry for Good Friday 1942, she writes: "there is just enough room for me to kneel down. Something I have been wanting to write down for days...A desire to kneel down sometimes pulses through my body, or rather it is as if my body has been meant and made for the act of kneeling."[36]

In a letter, she tells a friend of her discovery of the "Other." Her prayer is, "you have made me so rich, oh God... my life has become an interrupted dialogue with You, oh God, one great dialogue." Etty and her family perished in Auschwitz. She knew that she would never become the great artist she hoped to be. But she attests how she is "already secure in You, God...and that says everything, and there is no need for anything more."[37] She learned to kneel before the "[O]ther."[38]

Sixteen

Jacques Derrida (1930–2004): A Politics of Friendship

A Life

Jacques Derrida was born in Algeria (formerly a colony of France) into a Jewish family. After World War II, at age nineteen, he moved to Paris. He chanced to hear a radio broadcast about Albert Camus: philosopher, author of *The Stranger*, and later Nobel Prize winner. This led to his enrolling for philosophy classes at the *École Normale*. After his studies he divided his time between teaching in Paris and the United States and collaborating with American translators to produce various texts. Derrida became a famous media celebrity, with many books and television programs about him. There were also controversies like the "Cambridge honorary degree" affair, when he was initially denied the nomination by hostile academics. Nineteen analytic philosophers, including the American W.V.O. Quine, even sent a letter to *The Times* [London] claiming that he was insufficiently philosophical: "In the eyes of many philosophers... Mr. Derrida's work does not meet accepted standards of clarity and rigour.... When the effort is made to penetrate... [his thought] it becomes clear, to us at least, that, where coherent assertions are being made at all, these are either false or trivial."[1] In the end, Derrida was awarded the honorary doctorate in 1992. This is just an example of the controversy and fanfare that sometimes surrounded his academic career.

In the Beginning Was the "Mark"

Their labyrinthine nature makes Derridean texts notoriously difficult to read. He said that the term "deconstruction," probably one of his most famous and controversial terms, was a word "whose fortunes have disagreeably surprised me." Many took it to signify the "destruction" of all meaning, especially when applied to literature. English language departments in universities and schools, especially in the United States, championed this mistaken interpretation as the new and only way to carry out literary criticism.

For Derrida, the Western world is characterized by what he calls a "logocentrism of the Greco-Christian epoch." This perspective means that for rational human beings, "logos" or "meaning" is discoverable only as a definite fixed "presence." We simply need to unearth this "truth" in order to understand it. But here Derrida challenges us to think outside the box, that is, to peel back the hardboiled shell of our preconceptions. Accordingly, he contends that the greatest signification is not actually found in the spoken word or in some kind of discoverable "metaphysical presence" of meaning. Rather, as human beings we leave and make "traces" of *who* we are in this world. When it comes to understanding and discovering meaning in a text of whatever form, it is not about some logical and ethereal abstraction and deduction. When Derrida famously said, "There is nothing outside the text," he is reminding us that meaning is found in what human beings have written. A simple example is a poem. A poet may be dead but we as readers can still find meaning in the poem. This is what a poem is. If not, then it is not a poem. This means that the poetic writing's significance to a reader is not extinguished at the poet's demise. Therefore, a sonnet, for example, is actually where "nonpresent intentionality is most present."[2] This suggests that "significance" cannot just be trapped in a book. Significance goes beyond the earthly life of the author. Otherwise, meaning just ceases. Significance is, therefore, not contained nor is it retrievable from some kind of metaphysical and nebulous presence in an iCloud of significance! In other words, Derrida extols the virtue of a writing since it points "beyond its own ... [possible] finitude."[3] Indeed, here we might recall St. Bonaventure saying how vestiges of the divine are discoverable in creation. Similarly, as human beings, we leave our own distinguishable "marks" which tell their own story about *who* we are. "Meaning," therefore, is not an abstraction but actually "dwells among us." So the challenge is to read the "text" adequately.

Derrida, for instance, explains how in the "act" of "writing" we "produce a mark."[4] Here he has in mind not just actual physical writing as in a text, but pictorial, musical, and sculptural forms are also included. Cave art, as in the famous images painted in the Lascaux caves 17,000 years ago by our ancestors, comes to my mind. They express us not just as *homo faber* (humans as makers) but even more our identity as *homo spiritualis* (spiritual beings).

Even before we speak, we leave "marks" which symbolize our search for order. We leave smudges or traces of *who* we are, thereby differentiating ourselves as human beings from more "compact" and "mythological" understandings (as in certain myths). In this way, we are moving toward a greater appreciation of *who* we are in the world. Derrida, therefore, is suggesting that "writing," in fact, somehow precedes the "spoken" word, not the reverse. The act of writing, therefore, goes back to our originary experience as human beings. And as such, he says, it comes before the letter. In saying this, he wants to shake us out of our intellectual slumbers, waking us from simply sleepwalking, forgetting *who* we are as human persons.

Meaning Present in Absence

In my view, emergent here is a very keen insight into the incredible reality of our identity as human persons. In Derrida's opinion, humans cannot be understood in a one-dimensional way. We are far more complex, and the "meaning" of our "meaning" is equally multi-faceted. We must not, for example, let the "rags and bones" of mere soundbites of human language serve to encapsulate what it means to be *who* we are. Paradoxically, Derrida's thought-provoking reflections reveal how "meaning" is found not in "presence," but in "absence." He explains:

> For writing to be writing it must continue to "act" and to be readable even when what is called the author of the writing no longer answers for what he has written [that is, he or she is dead].... The situation of the writer is, concerning the written text, basically the same as that of the reader.[5]

Derrida has in mind the reality that in the event of writing, human beings have the capability of communicating significance beyond the "living present." This is what meaning really is, and this has enormous significance for us as human beings. The very act of writing breaks meaning free from a particular author or creator. Otherwise, it remains, as we might say, a mere dead-letter. This absence is not a nothingness but a presence, a transcendence, a "going-beyond" the present moment.

In Derrida's view, if writing is not this, then it is not writing at all. Consequently, the "absence" of the present author or "its current context of use" constitutes the actual *being* of "writing." An existential and historical example of the meaning of "absence" can be found in Abraham Lincoln's "Gettysburg Address." Lincoln speaks of how the land they have come to dedicate is hallowed not by those present but by the persons who are "absent." He says, "we [the living] can not consecrate—we can not hallow—this ground." It is the sacrifice of the ones not present that brings meaning to what is being done at Gettysburg. In *The Gift of Death*, Derrida readily recognizes that he could never personally measure up to this "level of infinite goodness nor up to the immensity of the gift, the frameless immensity that must in general define (*in*-define) a gift as such."[6] Nonetheless, we cannot deny the profound human "meaning" there is in "absence." Undeniably, the adage "absence makes the heart grow fonder" has deep human significance for every person, even Derrida.

The Vast Horizons of Political Friendship

In his later writings, such as *The Politics of Friendship*,[7] Derrida turned his attention to different themes. "Politics" and "friendship" might seem opposites, but they are not. "Political" brings to mind concepts like the role of government, sovereignty, citizenship, power, and representation. The idea of "friendship" rarely surfaces when we think of the world of politics. Indeed, over the last few years, most countries provide testimony to this heartrending reality. Consequently, what, we may well ask, has politics got to do with friendship?

Of course, Derrida is not the first philosopher to reflect on the subject of friendship. Actually, Aristotle looked on "friendship" as the highest form of political life. Derrida quotes many texts from Plato and Aristotle in which friendship is defined as the "essential virtue." In an earlier chapter, we have seen how Aristotle in the *Nicomachean Ethics* (1156a10–115b30) outlines three types of friendship: those based on utility and usefulness, on pleasure, and finally, friendships among people "who are good and alike in virtue" where "each alike wishes well to each other ... [and] they are good in themselves" (1156b7–9). Derrida calls these and other perspectives on friendships the "canonical views." He mentions how the Greek, Roman, Jewish, Christian, and Islamic cultures make hugely significant contributions to the theme. But he suggests that we rethink the whole question and go beyond our presupposed understandings. Derrida believes that "the history [and reality] of friendship cannot be reduced to these [canonic] discourses."[8]

He critically asks, "What would then be the politics which goes outside the closed boundaries of purely *'familial'* and *'fraternalist'* notions we might have?"[9] He seeks to provoke us into envisaging a new politics and asking what it would look like. Derrida does not want merely to develop a new theory of politics. Above all, he wants us to see the political dimension of life in a totally new way and live it from the perspective of "friendship." Everyone, he believes, would be a candidate to enter this new horizon of politics. It is not specific to any denomination, and this is its "truth." It requires us to think and speak in new ways. Derrida advises us that "friendship tells the truth — and this is always better left unknown" because it is actually unsettling to know the unknown. He writes how "friendship does not keep silence, it is preserved by silence."[10]

The Essence of Friendship

Democracy, Derrida says, certainly represents itself as facilitating "the possibility of *fraternization*." But what does this really mean? Regarding relations between siblings, he asks, "What happens when, in taking up the case of the sister, the woman is made a sister? And a sister a case of the brother?"[11] He explains how friendship is "*an act before being a situation*; rather, the *act of loving before being the state of being loved*." Friendship is essentially "the act and activity" of being a friend to the "other." He argues that "someone must love in order to know what loving means." Only in this way can "one ... know what being loved means." Derrida continually challenges, asking, "Friendship, the being-friend—what is that anyway? Well, it is to love *before* being loved. Before even thinking about what *loving, love, lovence* means, one must know that the only way to find out is by questioning first of all the act and the experience of loving rather than the state or situation of being loved."[12]

Derrida observes how "Aristotle therefore declares: as for friendship, it is advisable to love rather than to be loved."[13] Clearly, his priority is not on the theoretical but on the practical living out of the reality. Considering current events, it might seem that Derrida's thoughts are utopic and that the only possible [political] community is the impossible community. According to Derrida, if we leave it to brute facts, maybe it is all a dream. But "perhaps the impossible is the only possible chance of something new.... Perhaps friendship ... must honour [*fáire droit*] what appears impossible here."[14]

Democracy "To Come:" A New Fraternity

In *The Politics of Friendship*, Derrida often uses the phrase "democracy to come," but by it, he does not mean something occurring in the future. The "to come" is intended to refer to the right here and now. He says it has a "'to come' as a promise, as a duty, that is 'to come' immediately." Necessarily, this "to come" entails the insight of how "friendship" is the transformation of the concept of the political. Derrida readily admits that the "unconditionality of this [politics of friendship] is a frightening thing." He reminds us "democracy remains to come; this is its essence in so far as it remains." It will remain "indefinitely perfectible, hence always insufficient and future but at the same time it belongs to the time of promise." He asks, "when will we be ready for an experience of freedom and equality that is capable of respectfully experiencing that friendship, which ... [can be] ... measured up against its measurelessness?"¹⁵ This is all a part of unfolding the incredible reality of *who* we are. Fraternity is not a principle but constitutes the reality of *who* we are.

Some might consider Derridean perspectives on measuring up to the "measurelessness" of a fraternity-based politics to be totally utopian. Nonetheless, in 1996 a Movement for Unity in Politics began in Italy under the inspiration of Chiara Lubich. At a 2001 conference in Innsbruck for European mayors, she gave a talk, "The Spirit of Brotherhood in Politics, Key to the Unity of Europe and the World."¹⁶ During her presentation, Chiara explained:

> The response to a political vocation is before all else an act of brotherhood. In fact, one does not become politically active simply in order to resolve a problem.... In fact, politics seen as love creates and preserves those conditions that allow all other types of love to flourish.... Thus, *politics is the love of all loves* ... gathering people and groups into the unity of a common design so as to provide the means for each one to fulfill in complete freedom his or her specific vocation.¹⁷

In an address to British politicians at the Palace of Westminster, London (June 22, 2004), Lubich recalled how

> Igino Giordani, an Italian member of parliament ... wrote in his unique style: "When we cross the threshold of our home to plunge into the world, we cannot leave our faith hanging on the back of the door like a worn-out-hat.... Politics is charity in action, handmaid not ruler."¹⁸

Giordani had much experience of what he was talking about. Speaking about his own time in politics he once related:

> I was a fairly well-known polemicist at that time, and my writings and articles were now turned upside down

[after my conversion to a spirituality of unity]. The first transformation was to not view people primarily as adversaries, but first and foremost as human beings. We often forgot that we were always dealing with human beings, with brothers. Perhaps we spoke of that in our statements but when we were actually facing a Communist, someone from another party, we were instead raw, closed, enemies. Chiara's teachings, which taught us that we needed to see Christ in everyone and we were all brothers and sisters, transformed politics. It was a matter of seeking right over wrong, seeking collaboration not opposition.[19]

Derrida concludes his study on a politics of friendship with a plea: "When will we be ready for an experience of freedom and equality that is capable of respectfully experiencing that friendship which would at last be just, just beyond the law, and measured up against its measurelessness? O my democratic friends."[20] The answer is surely in our hands.

Seventeen

Pope Francis:
On the Forgotten Dimension of Fraternity

Assisi

On October 3, 2020, the vigil for the feast of St. Francis, Assisi seemed like the perfect stage and setting for the launch of Pope Francis's new encyclical *Fratelli Tutti*.[1] Yet, because of the pandemic, it turned out to be very low-key. The pope did not even preach or say much. There is a photograph of him elevating the host at the Mass he celebrated at the tomb of St. Francis. There were only a handful of people present. In one sense, this says it all. Even the pope knows that the written or spoken word has its own limits. Francis celebrating Mass at Assisi almost in silence in itself acknowledges that the truth of *who* we are as human beings is found only in the *One* who is beyond us. In human terms, anything written—even an encyclical—is really a saying of the unsayable. We cannot easily define *who* the "other" is, and to try is almost impossible.

Meeting the Sultan

At the beginning of the encyclical, Pope Francis mentions a meeting between the Sultan of Egypt Malik-el Kamil (1180–1238) and St. Francis in the Nile delta port city of Damietta, north of Cairo during the Crusades [3], over eight centuries ago. At first, St. Francis was forbidden by Cardinal Galvani of Albano to have such an encounter, but eventually, it happened. Nonetheless, Francis's mission seemed a failure since he did not convert anyone, let alone the Sultan. He was mostly laughed at by both sides. Throughout, however, he had no agenda but to love. His biggest conversions were, in fact, among the local Christian clergy and bishops. As Pope Francis says, "Francis felt himself a brother to the sun, the sea and the wind, yet he knew that he was even closer to those of his own flesh. . . . Francis's fidelity to his Lord was commensurate with his love for his brothers and sisters" [2, 3]. Indeed, throughout the encyclical, the pope refers to his own meeting in Abu Dhabi with the Grand Imam Al-Tayed, where they jointly declared, "God created all human beings equal in rights, duties and dignity, and has called them to live together as brothers and sisters" [5].

What Does Fraternity Mean?

Without a doubt, the forgotten dimension in the public domain is fraternity. The term is missing from political dictionaries and in much modern debate. Pope Francis turns to this theme since Christianity can make a unique contribution in developing an understanding of "what it means when we say 'brother,' when we call someone 'brother.'" We discussed this in the previous chapter when we considered Jacques Derrida's *The Politics of Friendship*. Even ancient Greek philosophers reflected on it. Plato says, "We and our fellow citizens are all brothers born of one another" (*Menexenos*, 279).

Therefore, fraternity actually establishes a boundary; if you are not united in a *polis*, then you are not a part of its brotherhood. Aristotle said, "Man is by nature a social animal; an individual who is unsocial . . . is either beneath our notice or more than human" (*Politics*). In the New Testament, however, Jesus sees "brothers" not in terms of an inner closed circle or blood-relationship understanding of fraternity, but as those who make the choice of God by saying "yes" to the will of God. He says, "No longer do I call you servants . . . but I have called you friends, for all I have heard from my Father I have made known to you" (Jn 15:15). Fraternity is based on a spiritual relationship, not just a phenomenon of nature. Pope Benedict XVI provides a most insightful and in-depth study of the theme in *The Meaning of Christian Brotherhood*, which, as I have said before, is well worth reading.²

Fraternity Seen Afresh

Pope Francis clearly recognizes that "this call to love [others] could be misunderstood" [62]. There can be false ideas about fraternity, and he plainly says that he is not proposing "an authoritarian and abstract universalism, devised or planned by a small group and presented as an ideal for the sake of levelling, dominating and plundering" [100]. Actually, Francis believes that "we forget the lessons of history, the teacher of life;" at our peril [34]. St. Paul reminded the Christians at Corinth of the "danger from false brethren [*pseudadelphois*]" (2 Cor. 11:26).

So fraternity is undoubtedly a controversial notion. The French philosopher August Comte, for example, proposed a completely worldly understanding based on the principle of altruism with one fundamental rule: "Live for the other person." These basic truths, inscribed in human nature, can be discovered on a purely rational level. In this way human beings can escape forever from any participation in the divine. But this leads to a hollow "humanism" in which the neighbor is treated as if containing no trace of the transcendent. Pope Francis, keenly aware of this danger, points to the life of the Trinity as our model of fraternity. He says, "If we go to the ultimate source of that love which is the very life of the triune God, we encounter in the community of the three divine Persons the origin and the perfect model for all life in society" [85]. Elaborating on this point, Maria Voce, a former president of the Focolare Movement, commenting on the publication of the encyclical, said that it is:

> In the Trinity, where unity and distinction coexist, where each person respects the other, each person makes room for the other, each person tries to bring out the other, each tries in a certain way to lose their own self completely so that the others can express themselves completely. In doing this they do not cancel themselves out; on the contrary they manifest their true and deepest identity.[3]

Thus, being "myself" as a person in no way annihilates the "other." St. Augustine said where we see love, we see the Trinity. Living *myself as another* is the realization of the life of the Trinity come to earth. It is the unfolding of a mystery called love, which is the giving of self. This giving of self is not accidental to our being but constitutive of us as persons. It is *who* we are. Without losing self, there is no going forward; "giving does not hold on tightly to what it has but gives up what it gives." We exist to go beyond ourselves.[4] And so "to be" is truly "to go" where no one but Christ has gone before.

The Hidden Power of Goodness

Nonetheless, the pope clearly says that we must embrace the world as it is "because there we will discover all the goodness that God has planted in human hearts. Difficulties that seem overwhelming are opportunities for growth, not excuses for glum resignation that can lead only to acquiescence" [78]. Francis gives a meditation on what he calls the parable about "a stranger on the road" (Lk 10: 25–37) [56 ff.]. This story has to do with "an age-old problem," that is, the "issue of human relationships" [57]. The parable does not allow "abstract moralizing"; it calls for a "decision" [67]. A definition will not answer the question "who is my neighbor?" Hence, Pope Francis suggests, it can be answered only by personal conversion. Jesus "asks us not to decide who is close enough to be our neighbor, *but rather that we ourselves become neighbors to all*" [80, my emphasis].

Francis points to the importance of "employing all the resources that the institutions of an organized, free and creative society" can actually generate [165]. He says, "even the . . . Samaritan . . . needed to have a nearby inn that could provide the help that he was personally unable to offer" [165]. The pope speaks positively about how it is important and noble "to place our hope in the hidden power of the seed of goodness we sow" [196]. In reading the texts of the New Testament, "We see how the early Christian communities, living in a pagan world marked by widespread corruption and aberrations" tried to live the Gospel [239]. So, the economic or political order that Christians build or contribute to truly matters. It is not an optional calling or merely an inconvenient truth or challenge. It is truly in this context that our intelligence, judgment, and human creativity unfold. It is a great divorce and an abolition of *who* we are as human persons to think and act otherwise. In this way, the "beauty . . . [of the] different faces of the one humanity that God so loves" can be realized [287].

We know of St. John's prologue in his Gospel: "In the beginning was the Word" (Jn 1:1). Pope Francis writes a kind of prelude too, observing,

> The world is always *being made*. Paul in his Letter to the Romans 8:22 says creation is groaning from birth pangs. God wants to bring forth the world with us, as partners, continually. He has invited us to join Him from the very beginning, in peaceful times and in times of crisis—at all times. It is not like we've been handed this thing all wrapped up and sealed: "Here, have the world."

In the Genesis account God commands Adam and Eve to be fruitful. Humankind has a mandate to change, to build, to master creation in the positive sense of creating from it and with it. So what is to come does not depend on some unseen mechanism, a future in which humanity is a passive spectator. No: we're protagonists, we're—if I can stretch the word—co-creators. When the Lord told us to go forth and multiply, to master the earth, he's saying: Be creators of your future.[5]

Eighteen

David Walsh: The Priority of the Person

A New Symphony

David Walsh is a professor of political philosophy at The Catholic University of America in Washington, DC. In my estimation, he is one of the most significant scholars in the English-speaking world on the theme of what it means to be a human person. Walsh, a native Dubliner, writes in a Joycean or Beckettian style, unfolding a very new perspective on the language of the person. His contribution is what I call a new symphony for a new world with many poignant movements. In this short chapter, we will try to listen in to the tones of his personalistic symphony by focusing on his book *The Priority of the Person,* since it is relevant to our overall focus in *Myself as Another.*

I remember well reading one of his earlier books, *Guarded by Mystery*, about the reality of the human person. He observed how the "human being is a process or a project, and it is up to each one of us to take charge of its development. We are responsible. We are free."[1] I sensed from this a new kind of freedom to be open in terms of discovering the truth of *who* we are as persons. But at the same time, I had a responsibility since I did not want unnecessarily to waste my time and end up just sleepwalking in reading materials that did not question me deeply enough. It is said that St. Augustine became a question (an enigma) to himself, and this is good advice because we cannot remain mere easychair travelers as we journey toward the heart of *who* we are. Emmanuel Levinas speaks of how "one must not sleep, one must philosophize."² He describes how we can often be intoxicated, walking around like somnambulists and dreaming as if we *know* it all. This is what I call the "bighead" syndrome. Indeed, in "The Deserted Village," the Irish poet Oliver Goldsmith, speaking of the village master, says "and still they gazed, and still the wonder grew, That one small head could carry all he knew."³ There is need for "an awakened heart" regarding measuring up to the mystery of *who* I am.

David Walsh's writings evoke in me such an "awakening," that is, to what Levinas terms the "transcendence in immanence" of the human person.⁴ In other words, as a human being, I am situated "outside of immanence" while still truly belonging to this world. It is somewhat like the Johannine sense of being "in the world but not of it" (Jn 17:11, 14–15). In a meditation, "The Attraction of Modern Times," Chiara Lubich catches this same reality when she explains how "this is the great attraction of modern times: to penetrate to the highest contemplation while mingling with everyone, one person alongside others . . . to lose oneself in the crowd in order to fill it with the divine, like a piece of bread dipped in wine."⁵ So, this is the "attraction" I am fascinated by in David Walsh's *oeuvre*.

An Economic "Overture": Flight of the Bumblebee

I read his writings while involved in my own PhD research about the development and recovery of an economic philosophical anthropology with special reference to the contribution of the Austrian School of Economics.⁶ Walsh's lifelong philosophical meditations and texts on the human person offered me keen insights into the reality I was trying to unfold and understand. Adapting Igino Giordani's insight mentioned in an earlier chapter, when we enter into the drama of daily existence, "we cannot leave off *who* we are as persons hanging it on the back of the door like a worn-out-hat." Indeed, Walsh's conception of the human person helped illuminate novel movements I discovered within economic thought aiming toward recapturing the centrality of the personal dimension in the economic process. Walsh outlines how in the modern philosophical revolution we can see a "turn to the person."[7] This is evident not just in the world of philosophy but also in the worlds of economics, politics, and the arts.

Indeed, throughout his writings, he observes how "the turn to the subject is the defining feature of the modern world."[8] Walsh describes Hegel, for example, as the inaugurator of the language of existence in modern philosophy. With Hegel, philosophy has become a living movement in which the priority of life over reflection emerges.[9] But many see Hegel as a *bête noir*! Nevertheless, according to Walsh, any "derailment into dogmatism" could now be avoided because, through Hegel's contribution, "the existential source had become unmistakably clear."[10] I think that Walsh's own dynamic "person-centric" analysis can likewise be applied to our understanding of the free economy and equally to the role of the person in such differing dimensions of the human drama as politics and the arts. The Walshian symphony of the person can, in fact, be performed and articulated in the various dimensions of existence. Walsh reveals the essential "face" of the person disclosed amid the world we inhabit. Concerning the economic dimension of life, he suggests that we forget at our peril what the free economy is based on. The Great Recession of 2008, for instance, was a huge shock to the system, yet it disclosed how "the whole vast network of interlocking [economic] transactions was in reality nothing more *than a web of hope*" and trust.[11] Walsh uses the image of how we are like the little bumblebee "whose flight is predicated on its unwillingness to listen to the" news that "its wings are too slight to support it."[12]

Everything is fine until turbulence hits and then we finally realize the forgotten or eclipsed personalistic foundations. We come face-to-face with what Paul Ricoeur calls our fragility which is a vital part of *who* we are as human persons.

In *Guarded by Mystery*, Walsh speaks of the human person as process.[13] Similarly, the free economy can be understood not as a machine or a system but as a process of continual discovery.[14] Walsh comments, for example, that "we create ourselves, not in the sense that we are the source of our own existence . . . but in the sense that we participate in the work of self-creation. That is the source of the dignity by which we surpass all other realities we know."[15] His theme is to focus on how "creativity" constitutes what it means to be a human being. This, I believe, can also help us unfold the drama of the truth of the person in economic life, something which I have tried to present through my writings in a very small way.

To "Unsuspecting Readers"

Let us now turn to his study, *The Priority of the Person*, published in 2020 by the University of Notre Dame Press. In the preface, Walsh admits that some of his previous studies were not easily comprehensible to "unsuspecting readers." The current volume presents, he hopes, "a more accessible inquiry into what it means to be a person."[16] In his earlier work, *After Ideology: Recovering the Spiritual Foundations of Freedom*, Walsh showed how it is not enough to begin merely by outlining and defending "the rightness of Christianity . . . and its view of human nature." This can remain a mere assumption on our part and therefore "not . . . [really] a discovery of experiential truth."[17] The challenge is that we must dig deeper to uncover and bring to light the existential reality of being human. In this way, our understanding necessarily develops as a living experience. In fact, in the very action of recovering it we become *who* we are as human beings. In the Walshian *oeuvre*, we see unfold a personal intellectual and spiritual journey along a person-centric pathway. At the same time, he believes that the "other" defines us as human beings. Thinking cannot be done alone; he says, "It is ever and always in the company of others."[18] His overall approach is not an investigation into words about words on the person but an invitation to join in the odyssey of engaging author and reader alike. By participating in Walsh's multidimensional voyage and exploring the illuminating insights he sets out, we will, in my view, see through the frayed clothing of the ideas we often dress others up in. Thereby, we allow the truth of *who* the other is to shine through.[19]

From Underneath the Rubble

In *After Ideology*, from underneath the rubble of the civilizational atrophy provoked by twentieth-century modern ideologies, Walsh draws out a map of recovery that charts the existential core of an ascent that can be traced within the human spirit. Fyodor Dostoevsky, Albert Camus, Aleksandr Solzhenitsyn, and Eric Voegelin, in his view, "exemplify the cathartic resolution of the crisis that finally allows the possibility of transcending it."[20] Then in *The Growth of the Liberal Soul*, he calls attention to how liberal politics, in fact, is ultimately dependent on such transcendent faith.[21] He asserts that liberal politics is "the translation of the transcendent worldview into the finite public realm."[22]

In *The Modern Philosophical Revolution: The Luminosity of Existence*, he gives a masterclass in a magnificent transformational reading of Kant, Hegel, Schelling, Nietzsche, Heidegger, Levinas, Derrida, and Kierkegaard. As I have suggested already, he sees them as inaugurating an existential shift away from a philosophical tradition concerned simply with the study of entities and concepts. Within these philosophers, he finds an existential meditation on the transcendent horizon within which we find ourselves.[23] I am reminded here once again of Levinas's reflections on the theme of "transcendence in immanence." Indeed, Walsh devotes a whole chapter to Levinas, who he says appreciates that "I participate in the infinite *not by possessing it but through infinite responsibility*."[24] In *Politics of the Person as the Politics of Being*, which appeared in 2016, Walsh sets out to work further on retrieving the missing link of the *relational person*, on which he was already working through the ongoing personalist symphony he was composing. Politics enjoys a very bad press these days and Walsh believes that focusing on the human person will have a restorative effect in terms of the theoretical dignity of the political. He concludes, in fact, that "politics is most complete when it has become politics of the person."[25]

On the Primacy of the Person

In *The Priority of the Person*, Walsh sets out various concrete examples of the philosophy of the person he has been investigating for years. In sixteen intellectually scintillating chapters, he outlines how if you want to address different questions like liberalism or the common good; if you want to know about the work of Eric Voegelin or reflect on the writings of Aleksandr Solzhenitsyn or Benedict XVI; if you wish to understand what happened in the great financial crisis of 2008, the best and most accessible way is to inquire into "*what it means to be a person*."[26]

As I said at the outset of this chapter, Walsh's work is part of a symphony on the human person, a modern yet classical symphony. Indeed, recall how Socrates's approach to a truly open inquiry unfolds by his asking Gorgias "who he is" [*Gorgias*, 447d]. For David Walsh, the answer is not a definition but is constituted as an "imperative of living."[27] In

Fratelli Tutti, Pope Francis makes a similar argument. And Walsh holds that the beginning of the beginning is that "the person, each person, is prior to all else that is."[28] This is not the declaration of metaphysical dogma but a discovery to be made. And because each person is unique and unrepeatable, the encounter with this truth happens ever anew. It is an existential, ongoing, breakthrough event. Gabriel Marcel spoke of this in a similar way in his language of "encounter."

Three Stages of Life

In Kierkegaardian fashion, Walsh speaks of the discovery of the priority of the person through three stages in life: the *political, philosophical*, and *historical* dimensions of existence. We discover the political in the immediacy of lived experience; the philosophical stage in the wonder of reflection on the already lived of the "not yet" reality; and the historical in the unfolding of these events, which, while remaining within space and time, are not limited within the historical horizon.

Significantly, Walsh begins by analyzing the political stage, with its initial breakthrough and differentiation in terms of discovering the primacy of the person. In the political realm, we as human beings discover how we are, so to speak, thrown into existence. We cannot postpone living or deciding since we have no time to "erect the principles by which a publicly representative order is affirmed."[29] In short, in this realm we have got to roll up our sleeves and "act" as persons. We do not necessarily have the easy option of non-participation. Here we see that *practice* or *praxis* comes "in advance of theoretical underpinnings." This is not unusual, Walsh says, since "reflection is always directed by what preexists it."[30]

Politics, in fact, is a response to the discovery that human beings have an "inner capacity for reflection." It is the Greeks who begin noticing these uniquely human capacities. Other breakthroughs happen in the Hebrew prophets, the Confucian sages, and the enlightened bodhisattvas. In this cultural, intellectual, and spiritual setting, as "the unique self-responsibility of the individual emerges," it becomes evident that "neither anointments nor appointments" surpass "independent judgment and truth."

Christianity too recognizes this personalistic reality but there is a constant struggle in its realization. In fact, Walsh argues, although the discovery of the "person" occurs within the Christian experience, it cannot be fully understood until the modern turn toward interiority.[31] It is also the case that words fail us in expressing the reality. Thus, we need an "intellectual and linguistic overhaul" to make sense of the whole discovery.[32]

David Walsh, in fact, is not simply referring to the linguistic shift required to account for the breakthrough; I believe that he already attempts to carry it out. He points out how we cannot "acknowledge the necessity of treating persons differently and then continue to speak of them in the language of things."[33] In a Beckettian sense but without Beckettian opacity, Walsh's linguistic and intellectual gift helps us move beyond the embarrassment and inadequacy of language, thereby allowing access to a more adequate treatment and expression of the mystery of the human person. In doing this, he does not remain prisoner to "the churn of stale words within the heart," but goes insightfully and with luminosity beyond them.[34] Speaking about the need for a new language, Walsh actually says:

> When a person expresses him- or herself [in words], the uppermost meaning is that of the person who exceeds what has been expressed. We might say that it is possible for human beings to express themselves because they never express themselves. Like God they remain hidden behind, yet present within, their creation. That

incommunicability that ultimately characterizes the person can be known only through the capacity of persons to recognize what cannot be recognized in each of them. Only persons can know persons.[35]

Widening Our Horizons: Seeing with "New Eyes"

So, Walsh's central contention is that the liberal political order is not a "house of cards" ready to easily fall. He finds good things within it. He says that its recognition of the inviolable dignity of persons and defense of human rights lets us glimpse "the inexhaustibility that each human being is." In this way, "what would otherwise be invisible, the infinity of the person, is rendered visible."[36] He views the language of rights favorably since it is after all an abbreviation for a far more extended knowledge of *who* the person is.[37] Some rather pessimistic modern commentators like Patrick Deneen (a professor of political science at the University of Notre Dame) and Richard Rorty (who was an American philosopher) perceive an ongoing collapse of liberal faith and its institutions. But Walsh sets out a much more optimistic approach. Notwithstanding their inherent weaknesses, liberal democracies remain, he says, oases preserving an ordered world turned toward "the preservation of individual dignity and respect."[38] He contends that the liberal political order contains essential fragments of coherence. Although liberal democracy may no longer know "the inspiration from which it lives," yet respect for "the dignity of the person is an oblique expression of reverence for that which is the source of human dignity."[39]

A novelty in Walsh's writings, very rare among academics, is how he reads political theorists, philosophers, and writers with what I call "new eyes." It is almost as if he makes a "pact of mercy" with each author as he discusses them. Indeed, addressing a group of Muslims on "love of neighbor,"

Chiara Lubich spoke about making a "pact of mercy," that is, of making an "amnesty" in our hearts.[40] Reading about other philosophers and thinkers through David Walsh's eyes makes me greatly aware of this. We can see such a "pact," for instance, in his discussion of John Rawls (another American philosopher), Søren Kierkegaard, and Aleksandr Solzhenitsyn's contributions. More than twenty-five years ago, in *The Growth of the Liberal Soul,* Walsh pointed out how liberal intellectuals "are more in the manner of lost souls who carry within them the flickering sense of that for which they seek."[41] Rawls's work might be initially interpreted as closed to the religious dimension of human existence, but Walsh unearths parameters that were worked out, he says, "within a theological-personalist horizon."[42]

Walsh sees Søren Kierkegaard as the culminating figure in the modern philosophical revolution in the turn to the subject and the passage to the person. He explains how Kierkegaard is, in fact, "the true originator of the philosophic movement known as 'personalism'" yet he is not seen as being within their ranks. Indeed, we have seen this already in our own previous discussion on Kierkegaard. David Walsh emphasizes how Kierkegaard "most thoroughly elaborates the interior movement by which . . . the person not only gains a foothold in the eternal but becomes indeed the substantial reality that is its indispensable concomitant. . . . The self is the self who not only expresses itself but binds itself."[43] The human person is, therefore, a threshold beyond "being." Each person is "the whole of being . . . each one stands outside of the whole of being . . . [and those] who know this already think within the horizon of the person."[44]

Historical Dimension:
Persons, Not Just "Froth and Bubble"

Concerning the historical breakthrough into the "priority" of the person, Walsh sees Aleksandr Solzhenitsyn's writings as transformative and emblematic of how history is transmuted; it is not simply a record of "the whirling buzzing confusion" of events. As the British philosopher R.G Collingwood remarks, history is not only "a scissors-and-paste affair"; rather, its meaning can be unfolded only "within a wider drama" *in which the participants are a part.*[45]

Human beings are not just froth and bubble in a pre-determined stream of history. In his chapter "Art and History in Solzhenitsyn's *Red Wheel,*" Walsh points out how "we are not responsible for history, only for our actions within it."[46] Indeed, human beings offer fresh possibilities "by which a new beginning becomes possible." This reflects Hannah Arendt's idea about "natality." In Solzhenitsyn's novel *November 1916*, the character Zinadia, for instance, exemplifies how "history does not have to be the perpetual round of oppression, and further oppression."[47] She had seduced a married man, abandoned her dying mother, and deserted her dying son for her lover. Nonetheless, in her personal confession (see chapter seventy-five of *November 1916*), she acknowledges her own responsibility, realizing that only by repentance and absolution can evil be overcome. In her "self-giving" act of repentance, history in itself unfolds "toward every human being at its irreplaceable center."[48] Father Alon, her confessor, sets out the broader horizons we all act and live within. He says: "In each of us there is a mystery greater than we realize. And it is in communion with God that we are able to catch a glimpse of it."[49]

David Walsh's works are a rediscovery, a recovery, and a glimpse of this dynamic ever-creative core of the human being. His writings search out how to adequately account for the "in-between" (*metaxic*) nature of the great drama of existence; in so doing, he uncovers what it means "to be" a person. Throughout *Myself as Another* and its chapters on the various philosophers and writers, we have seen how the intellectual and spiritual task is to participate in the breathtaking journey, both positively and critically, in order to arrive at the heart of the person. We cannot, as Samuel Beckett says, merely continue to mouth stale old words and utter jaded shibboleths in our discussions about what it means to be a person. We clearly need to articulate and use a new "*personed*" language in our times. But we will know what this new language is only when we begin to speak it and so are able to communicate with each other about it. *Myself as Another* is a project unfinished but begun, not a conclusion about *who* we are. It is surely about a "hope [that] does not disappoint."[50] As such, it is an unfinished symphony.

Afterword

Throughout the text, readers of *Myself as Another* have heard about the thoughts and words of various philosophers and writers. But I hope that the reader discovers them more as persons rather than just mere thinkers. I have not set out abstract theoretical considerations on the human person, but instead have issued an invitation to take part in the adventurous journey to the heart of *who* we are. The book is intended as a "gift." So, I hope, it speaks "heart-to-heart" to each of you. The French philosopher Jean-Luc Marion describes how the gift becomes a gift not when it is received but when the receiver (you, the reader) considers it as a gift "that is able to be accepted (acceptable)."[1] He also remarks on how for human beings, "giving . . . gives others the capacity for giving." If you find *Myself as Another* an "acceptable" meditation on *who* we are as persons, you might like to pass it on or recommend it to another person. Indeed, Jacques Derrida claimed a gift not received by anyone "is not a gift at all." Anticipating, of course, that this will not be the case for those who read this book.

Aleksandr Solzhenitsyn spoke of his "invisible allies," that is, those who secretly worked in the background on the copying, circulation, and smuggling of his writings from Russia to the West.[2] There were obviously no such difficulties in the publication of *Myself as Another*. But there is a hidden story to the writing of this book. And you can catch a glimpse of *who* these hidden allies are in the chapter "Paul Ricoeur: Oneself as Another." Ricoeur places emphasis on the capacities we have as human beings. He stresses how it is important to live in the reality of giving and receiving, even when we can no longer do anything, as in when we are ill or suffering. This is why for me, Blessed Chiara Badano is a marvelous example of what it means to be a realized human person.[3] Her life's motto, expressing her full acceptance of her final suffering and death—"If you want it, I want it too"—is a living out of some of the themes found in *Myself as Another*. Badano's story reminds me of Emmanuel Levinas's reflections on what he calls "substitution." This amazing human reality and possibility we can, I believe, see equally in my experience about the Berkeley tragedy and in the nurse's reaction to the suffering of one of the students. Because of the way she saw that the young student was living it, she said: "You'll grow on the inside as a person. . . You'll grow on the inside through all of this." Chiara Badano is ready to make the "substitution," and she addresses her prayer ("If you want it, I want it") to Jesus as the One who suffers for us. He is "substituting" for us. Chiara places herself in the shoes of the "other" which involves her exchanging herself for the other in what is most His own, His own responsibility. In the words of Jean-Luc Marion, it is "one degree of responsibility more, the responsibility for the responsibility of the other."[4] Levinas spoke of the "ontological absurdity" of the human, that is, when you come upon human beings living out the "priority of the other," which is what he calls a new type of "saintliness." The reflections in this book on Edith Stein and her experience of "empathy" exemplify this. A friend of Chiara Badano's once remarked, "At first we thought we'd visit her to keep her spirits up, but very soon we understood that, in fact, we were the ones who needed her. Her life was like a magnet drawing us to her." This is *who* we are as human beings.

In one of Solzhenitsyn's most renowned short stories, "Matryona's Home,"[5] Matryona is a long-suffering widow who overcomes every obstacle thrown at her in life with great nobility as a person. She tries to live in harmony with everyone, even her ungrateful family and neighbors. She, in fact, dies tragically as she is putting others "first" in a noble

Afterword

action. The narrator, Ignatich, the village teacher who takes up lodging with her, says at the end of the story: "We had all lived side by side with her and never understood that she was that righteous one without whom, as the proverb says, no village can stand. Nor any city. Nor our whole land."[6]

We live side by side with other persons and the enduring challenge is discovering *who* they and we are. Let us hope with an anticipation which does not surely disappoint us that we will live to appreciate the reality of "myself" as "another." Maybe it is the case that we will need "new eyes" but as Julian of Norwich said: "All will be well" as we journey to the heart of *who* we are.

Notes

Foreword

1. Maurice Friedman, *Martin Buber's Life and Work: The Early Years 1878-1923* (Boston, MA: Dutton, 1982), 5.
2. Martin Buber, *I and Thou* (Edinburgh: Clark, 1966) 4,8,11, 15.
3. Aubrey Hodes, *Encounter with Martin Buber* (London: Penguin 1975), 15.
4. Karol Wojtyła, *Person and Act and Related Essays*, trans. Grzegorz Ignatik (Washington, DC: The Catholic University of America Press, 2021), 407-414.
5. Edith Stein, trans. Kurt F. Reinhardt, *Finite and Eternal Being: An Attempt at an Ascent to the Meaning of Being* (Washington DC: ICS Publications, 2002), chapter 2, §7, 55.

One: Introduction: the search for *who* I am

1. See John McNerney *Wealth of Persons: Economics with a Human Face* (Eugene, OR: Cascade Books, 2016), for example, which aims at recapturing an adequate understanding of the acting person in the economic drama, one that measures up to the reality of *who* we are as persons.
2. *Confessions*, Book X, 27, 38. See (Hyde Park, NY: New City Press, 2001), 203.
3. Augustine, Book IV, 7,9, 62-63.
4. Hans Urs von Balthasar, *Explorations in Theology, V: Man Is Created* (San Francisco, Ignatius Press, 2014), 114.
5. Thomas Aquinas, 'Prologue,' in *St Thomas Aquinas on the Apostle's Creed*. See https://isidore.co/aquinas/Creed.htm, accessed January 11, 2024.
6. Thomas Nagel, *Mortal Questions* (Cambridge, MA: Cambridge University Press, 2008), 169.
7. Nagel, 170.
8. See https://www.luminarium.org/sevenlit/donne/meditation17.php, accessed May 16, 2023.
9. Plato, *Meno* in *Plato: The Collected Dialogues, Including the Letters*, eds. Edith Hamilton and Huntington Cairns, Bollingen Series LXXI (Princeton, NJ: Princeton University Press, 1989), 80a-d, 363.
10. David Walsh, *The Priority of the Person: Political, Philosophical, and Historical Discoveries* (Cambridge, MA: Cambridge University Press, 2020), 21.
11. Walsh, 21.

12. Emmanuel Levinas, *Unforeseen History*, trans. Nida Poller (Chicago, IL: University of Illinois Press, 2004), 128.
13. David Walsh, "Person Means Relation," St. Thomas Aquinas Lecture, University of Dallas, January 26, 2023 (unpublished). For a concise account of the historical development of the concept of the person the reader is referred to Hans Urs von Balthasar's "Person and Sexuality: On the Concept of Person" in *Explorations in Theology V: Man is Created*, 114–125. There is a clear and unique breakthrough in the Christian tradition into the understanding of "person." Boethius (480–524 AD) gives one of the first philosophical definitions in saying "a person is an individual substance of a rational nature." But with the twelfth-century Scottish Medieval philosopher and theologian Richard of St. Victor there is a new development in seeing that the term "person" means a spiritual subject which "goes out of (*ex*) and beyond itself" (119). Intimations of "person as relation" are found throughout history, but they somehow disappear. Von Balthasar observes how it takes "the vulgar atheistic materialism" of Ludwig Feuerbach to rediscover that there is no such "thing as an individual person who rests complete in himself alone" (121). A careful reading of St. Thomas Aquinas shows how "person" signifies "relation." In the *Summa*, Thomas says, "thus it is true to say that the name person signifies relation directly" (Q. 29, a.4). See https://www.ccel.org/ccel/a/aquinas/summa/cache/summa.pdf, accessed May 24, 2023.
14. Martin Buber, *I and Thou*, trans. Walter Kaufmann (New York: Simon & Schuster, 1996), 609.
15. John Macmurray, *Persons in Relation* (Atlantic Highlands, NJ: Humanities Press, 1979), 12. See also Esther MacIntosh, *John Macmurray's Religious Philosophy: What it Means to be a Person* (Abingdon, Oxford: Ashgate Publishing, 2011).
16. Von Balthasar, in "Person and Sexuality: On the Concept of Person," 114ff.
17. On a visit to Auschwitz, Pope John Paul II described how it was constructed "*to trample underfoot radically*, not only love, but all signs of human dignity… of humanity." See John McNerney, *John Paul II: Poet and Philosopher* (London: T&T Clark, 2005), 63.
18. Macmurray, *Persons in Relation*, 28.
19. Macmurray, 44-63. Hans Urs von Balthasar in *Unless You Become Like This Child*, trans. Erasmo Leiva-Merikakis (San Francisco, CA: Ignatius Press, 1991) gives a moving meditation on the theme of spiritual childhood. The Greeks and Romans viewed childhood as a "not-yet" stage, but for Jesus, this is not so. In fact, the ways of a child open us to the original dimensions of *who* we are (12). Von Balthasar outlines how "to be a child means to owe one's existence to another" (49).
20. Macmurray, *Persons in Relation*, 61. The Spanish philosopher Jesús Morán makes an interesting distinction between "relationship" and "relationality." He says, "having many relationships is not necessarily an indicator of rela-

tionality." Morán gives the example of a how a cloistered nun may not have many relationships and yet because she is open "to the infinite" she is rich in "relationality." Another example he gives is that of an unconscious patient. If we hold that the person is primarily relationship, "meaning the capacity to build relationships" then a comatose person would not have "the right to live because of not being able to have relationships with others." But Morán observes at the root of a person is "relationality, which does not need relationships in order to exist because it comes before them." See https://www.focolare.org/en/2016/08/06/jesus-moran-relazione-e-relazionalita/, accessed May 23, 2023. The movie *The Diving Bell and the Butterfly* about the renowned *Elle* magazine editor Jean-Dominique Bauby who was paralyzed after a stroke tells the remarkable story of how he lived "relationality."

21. Walsh, *Priority of the Person*, 87–88.
22. Walsh, 17.
23. Plato, *Meno*, 80e, 363.
24. John Henry Newman, *An Essay in Aid of a Grammar of Ascent* (Notre Dame, IN: University of Notre Dame Press, 1992), chapter IV, 3.
25. John Henry Newman, *The Idea of a University* (Notre Dame, IN: University of Notre Dame Press, 2013), 52–53.
26. Søren Kierkegaard, *The Journals of Kierkegaard*, trans. Alexander Dru (New York: Harper & Brothers, 1959), 44.
27. Ludwig Wittgenstein, *Tractatus Logico-Philosophicus*, trans. C.K. Ogden (Garden City, NY: Dover Publications, 1999), (7), 108.
28. Wittgenstein, 4.112, 52.
29. Macmurray, *Persons in Relation*, 17.
30. Wittgenstein, *Tractatus Logico-Philosophicus*, (4.0020, 44).
31. See Jenny Teichman, "Wittgenstein on Persons and Human Beings," in *Understanding Wittgenstein, Royal Institute of Philosophy Lectures, Volume Seven, 1972–1973* (New York: St Martin's Press, 1974), 133–148. Teichman says the "overall conclusion" taken from Wittgenstein is that language depends on the possibility of common "forms of life" which is based on "the existence of human beings regarded as members of" a group. She emphasizes how this is made up "not of a single person, nor even of several separate persons, but rather, of people…having not only common characteristics but also common (mutual) responses, interactions etc." (145).
32. Dietrich Bonhoeffer, *Letters and Papers from Prison*, trans. Isabel Best et al (Minneapolis, MN: Fortress Press, 2015), 448.
33. Bonhoeffer, 217–218.
34. Christos Yannaras, *Person and Eros*, trans. Norman Russell (Brookline, MA: Holy Cross Orthodox Press, 2007), 115.
35. Yannaras, 20.

36. Alfred Delp. SJ, *Prison Writings* (Maryknoll, NY: Orbis Books, 2004), xxvii.
37. Viktor E. Frankl, *Man's Search for Meaning*, trans. Ilse Lasch (Boston, MA: Beacon Press, 2006), 76. Frankl adapts Nietzsche's motto "if we have our own *why* of life, we shall get along with almost any how," which comes from *Twilight of the Idols*. See *The Portable Nietzsche Reader*, ed. and trans. Walter Kaufman (New York: Penguin Books, 1982), 468.
38. Frankl, *Man's Search for Meaning*, 77–78.
39. Hannah Arendt, *Eichmann in Jerusalem: A Report on the Banality of Evil* (New York: Penguin Books, 2006).
40. Arendt, 135.
41. Hannah Arendt, *The Human Condition* (Chicago, IL: The University of Chicago Press, 2018), 5, my emphasis.
42. Arendt, *Eichmann in Jerusalem*, 5.
43. Arendt's approach is not unique. Karol Wojtyla's (St. John Paul II) *Person and Act and Related Essays*, trans. Grzegorz Ignatik (Washington, DC: The Catholic University of America Press, 2021) offers an in-depth philosophical investigation into how action is revelatory of what it means to be a human person. In the field of economics, the Austrian and Bologna schools place emphasis on human action and the role of the entrepreneur in business. See McNerney, *Wealth of Persons: Economics with a Human Face* (Eugene, OR: Cascade Books, 2016).
44. Arendt, *Eichmann in Jerusalem*, 179.
45. Emmanuel Levinas, *Alterity and Transcendence*, trans. Michael B. Smith (New York: Columbia University Press, 1999), 27.
46. Levinas, 56.
47. Levinas, 126.
48. H.Y. Jung, "The Logic of the Personal: John Macmurray and the Ancient Hebrew view of Life," *The Personalist*, 1966, Vol. 47, 532-46.
49. Emmanuel Levinas, *Unforeseen History*, 127.
50. Karol Wojtyla's reflections on the Marxian analysis were somewhat like Weil's considerations. See his essay "Participation or Alienation," in *Person and Act*, 514–531.
51. Simone Weil, *Late Philosophical Writings*, trans. Eric O. Springsted and Lawrence E. Schmidt (Notre Dame, IN: University of Notre Dame Press, 2015), 33.
52. Weil, *Gravity and Grace* (London: Routledge, 2002), 12.
53. Weil, *Late Philosophical Writings*, 62.
54. Weil, 62. Chiara Lubich uses the image of "pruning" as helping us grow in love of the "other." She writes "Yes, we have to 'cut away' in order to be more open, more disposed to love. We must 'do some pruning' in order to love better." See Lubich, *The Art of Loving* (Hyde Park, NY: New City Press, 2010), 76.

55. Bernard J. F. Lonergan, S.J., *Method in Theology* (London: Darton, Longman & Todd, 1972), 130.
56. Paul Ricoeur, *Philosophy, Ethics, and Politics*, trans. Kathleen Blamey (Cambridge, UK: Polity Press, 2020), 129.
57. Ricoeur, *Oneself as Another* (Chicago, IL: The University of Chicago Press, 1992), 185.
58. Ricoeur, *The Philosophy of Paul Ricoeur: An Anthology of His Work* (Boston, MA: Beacon Press, 1978), 241.
59. Catherine declared "My nature is a flame…I am the fire and you are the sparks…If you really are what you are supposed to be you will set fire to all Italy." See Igino Giordani, *Catherine of Siena: Fire and Blood*, trans. Thomas J. Tobin (Milwaukee, MI: Bruce Publishing Company, 1959), 139.
60. Jacques Derrida, *The Politics of Friendship*, trans. George Collins (London: Verso, 2020).
61. See Aaron Wessman, *The Church's Mission in a Polarized World* (Hyde Park, NY: New City Press, 2023).
62. Jacques Derrida, *Margins of Philosophy*, trans. Alan Bass, (Chicago, IL: University of Chicago Press, 1982).
63. See Geoffrey Bennington, "Politics and Friendship: A Discussion with Jacques Derrida," Centre for Modern French Thought, University of Sussex, December 1, 1997. See http://hydra.humanities.uci.edu/derrida/pol+fr.html, accessed May 27, 2023.
64. Derrida, *The Politics of Friendship*, 305.
65. Joseph Ratzinger, *The Meaning of Christian Brotherhood* (San Francisco, CA: Ignatius Press, 1966).
66. Ratzinger, 66–67.
67. Alexis Tocqueville, *Democracy in America*, trans., Harvey C. Mansfield and Delba Winthrop (Chicago, IL: The University of Chicago Press, 2000), Volume Two, Part Two, chapter 5, 489.
68. Derrida, "Politics and Friendship: A Discussion…." The reader is also referred to the very fine study by John von Heyking, *The Form of Politics: Aristotle and Plato on Friendship* (Montreal: McGill-Queen's University Press, 2016).
69. See Tunku Varadarajan, "Opinion, The Weekend Interview with Henry Kissinger: The Great Strategist Turns 100," *The Wall Street Journal*, May 27–28, 2023. Kissinger said what he sees when he looks at the world today is "disorder…almost all major countries…are asking themselves about their basic orientation."
70. See a collection of essays on the theme of "fraternity" as the forgotten dimension in contemporary political thought in Italian *Il Principio Dimenticato: La Fraternità nella Riflessione Politologica Contemporanea*, ed. Antonio Maria Baggio (Rome: Città Nuova, 2007). See also Antonio M. Baggio, "The Forgotten

Principle: Fraternity in its Public Dimension," *Claritas, Journal of Dialogue & Culture*, Vol. 2, No. 2 (October 2013).

71. Pope Francis, *Let us Dream: The Path to a Better Future* (New York, Simon & Schuster, 2020), 98–99).
72. Pope Francis, 107. My emphasis.
73. Pope Francis, *Fratelli Tutti: Encyclical Letter on Fraternity and Social Friendship*, (141).See https://www.vatican.va/content/francesco/en/encyclicals/documents/papa-francesco_20201003_enciclica-fratelli-tutti.html, accessed January 11, 2024. See John McNerney, "Patriotism in light of Fratelli tutti," in *Living City Magazine*, Hyde Park, NY, July–August 2023, volume 62, number 5.
74. Perry Link and Wu Dazhi, *I Have No Enemies; The Life and Legacy of Liu Xiaobo* (New York: Columbia University Press, 2023), 3–4, my emphasis.
75. Link and Dazhi, 18.
76. Václav Havel, *Open Letter: Selected Prose 1965–1990* (London: Faber and Faber, 1992), 125–214.
77. Havel, 210.
78. Chiara Lubich, *The Art of Loving*, 59. I refer the reader to Lubich's thoughts on "fraternity" and its political prospects in "The Charism of Unity and Politics." See Chiara Lubich, *Essential Writings: Spirituality, Dialogue, Culture*, eds. Tom Masters and Callan Slipper (Hyde Park, NY: New City Press, 2007), 230–268.
79. Pope Francis, *Fratelli Tutti*, (68–78).
80. Karl Marx makes the remark in the *Economic and Philosophic Manuscripts of 1844*. See *The Marx-Engels Reader*, ed. Robert C. Tucker (New York: Norton & Norton & Company, 1978), 66.
81. Plato, *Apology*, 38a. See in *Plato: The Collected Dialogues*.
82. David Walsh, *Politics of the Person as the Politics of Being* (Notre Dame, IN: University of Notre Dame Press, 2016).
83. Walsh, 16.
84. See William Butler Yeats, "September 1913." The poem reads: "What need you, being come to sense, / But fumble in the greasy till/ And add the halfpence to the pence...." *The Poems* (London: Everyman's Library, 1990), 159.
85. David Walsh, *The Priority of the Person: Political, Philosophical, and Historical Discoveries* (Notre Dame, IN: University of Notre Dame Press, 2020), 26. See Walsh's penetrating discussion on "Rights as an epiphany of the Person," in *Politics of the Person*, 246–256.
86. Walsh, *Politics of the Person*, 235.

Two: Daniel O'Connell and Frederick Douglass: A Narrative on "Fraternity"

1. I refer readers to David. W Blight, *Frederick Douglass: Prophet of Freedom* (New York: Simon & Schuster, 2018).

2. See *Narrative of the Life of Frederick Douglass, An African American Slave & Incidents in the Life of a Slave Girl*, Harriet Jacobs (New York: The Modern Library, 2000).

3. Patricia J. Ferreira, "Frederick Douglass and the 1846 Dublin Edition of His Narrative," *New Hibernia Review* 5, no. 1 (2001): 53–67.

4. See "Preface to the Second Dublin Edition" of the *Narrative of the Life of Frederic Douglas* in *Narrative of the Life of Frederick Douglass, An American Slave, Written by Himself*, eds. William L. Andrews and William S. McFeely, (New York: W.W. Norton & Company, 1997), 97.

5. Patrick M. Geoghegan, *Liberator: The Life and Death of Daniel O'Connell, 1830-1847* (Dublin: Gill & Macmillan, 2013). Readers can consult the writings of the eminent Irish economic historian Colm O'Gráda on the Irish Famine. See his *The Great Irish Famine (New Studies in Economic and Social History,* Series Number 7 (Cambridge, UK: Cambridge University Press, 1995).

6. *Narrative of the Life of Frederic Douglas*, Norton Critical Edition, 32–33. This is the edition I cite from unless otherwise stated. Hereafter, *Narrative*.

7. Charles Dickens was a parliamentary reporter at the British Parliament during this time and considered most politicians as pompous, speaking "sentences with no meaning in them." But Dickens said this was not the case with O'Connell. During one speech given by O'Connell at Westminster, it is said that Dickens was "compelled to down his pen, as tears flowed when the Member for Ireland spoke." See "Dickens Reports O'Connell: A Legend Examined," William J. Carlton, *Dickensian*, London, Vol, 65, Issue 358, May 1, 1969, 95.

8. *Narrative*, 35–36, my emphasis.

9. Pope Francis, *Fratelli Tutti*, (24).

10. Laurence Fenton, *Frederick Douglass in Ireland: The Black O'Connell* (Leicester, UK: Ulverscroft Press, 2014), 74.

11. Cited in Patricia Ferreira, "All But 'A Black Skin and Wooly Hair:' Frederick Douglass's Witness of the Irish Famine," in *American Studies International*, June 1999, Vol. 37, No. 2, 69–83. See also letter to Garrison: https://docsouth.unc.edu/neh/douglass/support12.html, accessed May 31, 2023.

12. See as cited in Ferreira, "All But 'A Black Skin and Wooly Hair.'"

13. Douglass, *Life and Times of Frederick Douglass, Written by Himself*, in *Frederick Douglass: Autobiographies* (New York: The Library of America, 1994), 682–683.

14. Douglass, 682.

15. Douglass, 683.
16. Fenton, *Frederick Douglass in Ireland*, 117–118. See also *Frederick Douglass in Ireland: In His Own Words, Volume I & II*, ed. Christine Kinealy (New York: Routledge, 2018), 216.
17. Fenton, 118–119.
18. Douglass, *My Bondage and My Freedom*, 225 (in *Autobiographies*).
19. Douglass, 225–226.
20. Douglass, 226.
21. Douglass, 227-228.
22. Douglass, 228.
23. Douglass, 227–228.
24. Douglass, 229.
25. Douglass, 229.
26. Douglass, 230.
27. Douglass, 233.
28. See 'Letter to His Old Master' in *My Bondage and My Freedom*, 264–270.
29. Douglass, *My Bondage* 265–266. My emphasis.
30. Douglass, 270.
31. See https://www.gilderlehrman.org/sites/default/files/inline-pdfs/T-07484-06-final.pdf, accessed June 1, 2023.
32. Douglass, *My Bondage and My Freedom*, 235.
33. See Aleksandr Solzhenitsyn, *The Gulag Archipelago: An Experiment in Literary Investigation, Volume 3*, Part IV, Chapter 1 in *The Solzhenitsyn Reader: New and Essential Writings 1947–2005*, eds. Edward E. Ericson, Jr. and Daniel J. Mahoney (Wilmington, DE: ISI Books, 2006), 265–266.

Three: St. John Henry Newman: "Heart to Heart" as an Educational Ideal

1. For the whole background to Newman's *The Idea of a University* and the founding of the Catholic University of Ireland, I refer the reader to Ian Ker, *John Henry Newman* (Oxford: Oxford University Press, 2010), 376–416.
2. John Henry Cardinal Newman, *The Idea of a University*, ed. Martin J. Svaglic (Notre Dame, IN: Notre Dame University Press, 2013). Cited hereafter as *Idea*.
3. Newman, 77.
4. Newman, 75.
5. Newman, 77.
6. Newman, 90–91.

Notes

7. David Walsh, "John Henry Newman: A Step Closer to Sainthood for a Modern Intellectual." See https://voegelinview.com/a-step-closer-to-sainthood/, accessed June 1, 2023.
8. Aristotle, *The Nicomachean Ethics* (1098a8–15).
9. Newman, *Idea*, 159.
10. Newman, 109.
11. Newman, 110–111.
12. Newman, 134–135.
13. Walsh, "John Henry Newman."
14. Walsh, 52–53.
15. For an in-depth study of Newman's "personalist" perspectives, I recommend the study by John F. Crosby. See *The Personalism of John Henry Newman* (Washington, DC: The Catholic University of America Press, 2016).
16. Newman, *Apologia Pro Vita Sua* (London: Collins, 1959), 92–93, my emphasis.
17. Newman, 93.
18. Newman, *Historical Sketches*, Volume III, "The Rise and Progress of Universities," Chapter 6, and "Discipline and Influence." See http://www.newmanreader.org/works/historical/volume3/index.html#contents, accessed December 23, 2019.
19. Newman, *Idea*, 181.
20. Newman, 52–53.
21. Newman, 57.
22. Hayek, "The Dilemma of Specialization," in *Studies in Philosophy and Economics* (London: Routledge & Kegan Paul, 1967), 123.
23. Newman, *Idea*, 247–248.
24. David Walsh, *Guarded by Mystery: Meaning in a Postmodern Age* (Washington, DC: The Catholic University of America Press, 1999), 26.
25 See HRH, The Prince of Wales, "John Henry Newman: The Harmony of Difference," *L'Osservatore* Romano, October 12, 2019. See https://www.vaticannews.va/en/vatican-city/news/2019-10/newman-canonization-prince-charles-editorial-britain.html, accessed June 4, 2023.
26. Newman, *Apologia*, 380. Newman aided cholera victims many times. His bishop Dr. Ulathorne thanks him for remaining in Bilston, Birmingham "till the worst [of the cholera outbreak] was over." See also Peter Conley, "John Henry Newman's Pandemic Ministry: A Balm for the Bereaved," https://www.newmanreview.org/john-henry-newman-s-pandemic-ministry-a-balm-for-the-bereaved/, accessed June 4, 2023.

Four: Søren Kierkegaard: Stages on Life's Way

1. Kierkegaard, *Either/Or, Part II*, eds. Howard V. Hong and Edna H. Hong (Princeton, NJ: Princeton University Press, 1990), 168.
2. Kierkegaard, 167.
3. Kierkegaard, 168.
4. Kierkegaard, 168–169.
5. Kierkegaard, *The Journals of Kierkegaard*, trans. and ed. Alexander Dru (New York: Harper & Brothers, 1959), 44.
6. Kierkegaard, 43.
7. Kierkegaard, 45.
8. Kierkegaard, 45.
9. Kierkegaard, 42–43.
10. Kierkegaard, *Stages on Life's Way*, trans. and eds. Howard V. Hong and Edna H. Hong (Princeton, NJ: Princeton University Press, 1991), 476.
11. Kierkegaard, 476–477, my emphasis.
12. Kierkegaard, 476.
13. See David Walsh, "Why Kierkegaard is the Culminating Figure of the Modern Philosophical Revolution," in *The Priority of the Person*, 225.
14. Walsh, 225.
15. Walsh, 225.
16. Kierkegaard, *Fear and Trembling: Dialectical Lyric by Johannes de Silentio*, trans. Alasdair Hannay (London: Penguin Books, 2003), 88. I quote from the Penguin edition throughout the book. See also *Fear and Trembling and Repetition*, eds. and trans. Howard V. Hong and Edna H. Hong (Princeton, NJ: Princeton University Press, 1983).
17. Kierkegaard, *Fear and Trembling*, 90.
18. Walsh, *Priority*, 226.
19. Walsh, 226.
20. Kierkegaard, *Fear and Trembling*, 97.
21. Walsh, *Priority*, 230-233.
22. Kierkegaard, *Works of Love*, trans. and eds. Howard V. Hong and Edna H. Hong (Princeton, NJ: Princeton University Press, 1998), 21.
23. Kierkegaard, 63.
24. Kierkegaard, 89, my emphasis.
25. Kierkegaard, 89.
26. When friends visit me in Washington, DC, I often bring them to see Jan van Eyck's "The Annunciation" (c. 1434) at the National Gallery of Art. What

strikes me about the painting is how Mary's humility is highlighted. She is the expert on "nothingness." It is through her "yes" that she sets off a whole symphony of unfinished "yesses."

27. Kierkegaard, *Fear and Trembling*, 93, my emphasis. In the Princeton edition, see page 65.
28. Chiara Lubich, *Essential Writings*, 46, my emphasis.
29. Kierkegaard, *The Journals*, 233.
30. *Paradise: Reflections on Chiara Lubich's Mystical Journey*, ed. Donald W. Mitchell (Hyde Park, NY: New City Press, 2020), 225.

Five: Ludwig Wittgenstein: A Personal Odyssey

1. Ray Monk, *Ludwig Wittgenstein: The Duty of Genius* (New York: Penguin Books, 1991), 130.
2. Ibid., 173.
3. Wittgenstein, *Tractatus Logico-Philosophicus*, trans. C.K. Ogden (Garden City, NY: Dover Publications, 1999), 22.
4. Wittgenstein, 27.
5. Wittgenstein, *Philosophische Untersuchungen: Philosophical Investigations*, trans. G.E.M. Anscombe, P.M.S. Hacker and Joachim Schulte (Oxford, UK: Blackwell Publishing, 2009). 123. The numbering refers to the proposition numbers in *Philosophical Investigations*.
6. Wittgenstein, 123–126.
7. Wittgenstein, 129.
8. Wittgenstein, 308.
9. Wittgenstein, 304.
10. Wittgenstein, 309.
11. *Tractatus Logico-Philosophicus*, 6.41.
12. Wolfram Eilenberger, *The Time of the Magicians: Wittgenstein, Benjamin, Cassirer, Heidegger and the Decade that Reinvented Philosophy*, trans. Shaun Whiteside (New York: Penguin Books, 2021), 41.
13. Fergus Kerr, *"Work on Oneself:" Wittgenstein's Philosophical Psychology* (Washington, DC: The Catholic University of America Press, 2008), 53.
14. *Collected Works of Bernard Lonergan, Volume 3, Insight: A Study of Human Understanding*, eds. Frederick E. Crowe and Robert M. Doran (Toronto: University of Toronto Press, 2013), 437.
15. Wittgenstein, *Culture and Value*, trans. Peter Winch (Chicago, IL: The University of Chicago Press, 1984), 32e.
16. Wittgenstein, 33e.

17. Pope John Paul II, *Fides et Ratio: On the Relationship between Faith and Reason* (Boston, MA: Pauline Books and Media, 1998), 7.
18. Wittgenstein, *Culture and Value*, 78e.
19. Wittgenstein, 48e.
20. Martin Heidegger, *Basic Writings*, ed. David Farrell Krell (New York: Harper Collins, 2008), 217, 219.
21. See David Walsh, *The Modern Philosophical Revolution: The Luminosity of Existence* (New York: Cambridge University Press, 2008), 232–290.
22. Kerr, "Work on Oneself," 54.
23. Wittgenstein, *Philosophical Investigations*, 66.
24. Wittgenstein, 66.
25. Wittgenstein, 67.
26. Wittgenstein, *Culture and Value*, 31e.
27. Kerr, "Work on Oneself," 54–55.
28. Helen Keller, *The Story of My Life* (New York: Dover Thrift Editions, 1996), 12, my emphasis.
29. Walsh, *The Modern Philosophical Revolution*, 318.
30. Wittgenstein, *Philosophical Investigations*, 531.
31. Brendan Purcell, *From Big Bang to Big Mystery: Human Origins in the Light of Creation and Evolution* (Hyde Park, NY: New City Press, 2012), 233.
32. Wittgenstein, *Philosophical Investigations*, 243–315.
33. Walsh, *The Modern Philosophical Revolution*, 318.
34. A movie was made on the whole Helen Keller experience. See *The Miracle Worker* directed by Arthur Penn.
35. See Jenny Teichman, "Wittgenstein on Persons and Human Beings," in *Understanding Wittgenstein, Royal Institute of Philosophy Lectures, Volume Seven, 1972–1973* (New York: St. Martin's Press, 1974), 133–148.

Six: Gabriel Marcel: Philosopher of "Presence"

1. Pope Francis, *Fratelli Tutti*, 63.
2. See *The Mystery of Being, Volume I: Reflection and Mystery (Gifford Lectures, 1949–1950)*, trans. G.S. Fraser (South Bend, IN: St. Augustine's Press, 2001) and *Mystery of Being, Volume II: Faith and Reality (Gifford Lectures 1949–1950)* trans. Rene Hague (South Bend: IN: St. Augustine's Press, 2001). Marcel met with the Scottish personalist John Macmurray while he was in Edinburgh giving the Gifford lectures.
3. Peter Salmon, *An Event, Perhaps: A Biography of Jacques Derrida* (London: Verso Books, 2020), 34–35, my emphasis.

Notes

4. Marcel, *Being and Having: An Existentialist Diary* (New York: Harper & Row, 1965).
5. *The Philosophy of Gabriel Marcel: The Library of Living Philosopher*, Volume XVII, eds. Paul Arthur Schilpp and Lewis Edwin Hahn (La Salle, IL: Open Court, 1991), 250.
6. See *A Gabriel Marcel Reader*, ed. Brendan Sweetman (South Bend, IN: St. Augustine's Press, 2011), 127.
7. *The Philosophy of Josiah Royce*, ed. John K. Roth (New York: Thomas Y. Crowell Company, 1971), 253.
8. Marcel, *The Philosophy of Gabriel Marcel*, 124.
9. Marcel, 124.
10. Marcel, *Homo Viator: Introduction to the Metaphysic of Hope*, trans. Emma Craufurd and Paul Seaton (South Bend, IN: St Augustine's Press, 2010).
11. Marcel, 296.
12. Marcel, *The Philosophy of Gabriel Marcel*, 61, my emphasis.
13. Marcel, 65, my emphasis.
14. Marcel, "Concrete Approaches to Investigating the Ontological Mystery," in *Gabriel Marcel's Perspectives on the Broken World*, trans. Katherine Rose Hanley (Milwaukee, WI: Marquette University Press, 2008), 172–173. Hereafter, *Gabriel Marcel's Perspectives*.
15. Marcel, 174.
16. Marcel, 174.
17. Marcel, 181. Eric Voegelin speaks of "an *anamnesis*, a recollection of decisive experiences" from his childhood. He describes how it is these types of experiences "of participation in various areas of reality" which constitute "the horizon of existence." He understands the chief task of philosophy as opening us up to recapturing this reality. See *The Collected Works of Eric Voegelin, Volume 34, Autobiographical Reflections*, ed. Ellis Sandoz (Columbia, MO: University of Missouri Press, 2006), 97.
18. *Gabriel Marcel's Perspectives*, 182, my emphasis.
19. Marcel, 183.
20. See John McNerney, *John Paul II: Poet and Philosopher* (London: T & T Clark, 2004).
21. See *A Gabriel Marcel Reader*, 73–74.
22. Marcel, *Gabriel Marcel's Perspectives*, 183.
23. Marcel, *A Gabriel Marcel Reader*, 75.
24. Marcel, *Creative Fidelity*, trans. Robert Rosthal (New York: Fordham University Press, 2002), 47.
25. Marcel, *A Gabriel Marcel Reader*, 128–129.

26. Marcel, *Gabriel Marcel's Perspectives*, 190, my emphasis.
27. Marcel, 191, my emphasis.
28. Marcel, *Homo Viator*, 140, my emphasis.
29. Chiara Lubich, *Essential Writings*, 86.
30. Lubich, 142.
31. Marcel, *Being and Having*, 138–139.
32. Marcel, *Homo Viator*, 190.
33. Marcel, *Thou Shall Not Die*, trans. Katharine Rose Hanley (South Bend, IN: St. Augustine's Press, 2009), 65.

Seven: Edith Stein: Stairway to the "Other"

1. Waltraud Herbstrith, *Edith Stein: The Untold Story of the Philosopher and Mystic Who Lost Her life in the Death Camps of Auschwitz*, trans. Father Bernard Bonowitz, O.C.S.O (San Francisco, CA: Ignatius Press, 1992), 40. I refer readers to Robert McNamara's study *The Personalism of Edith Stein: A Synthesis of Thomism and Phenomenology* (Studies in the Carmelite Tradition), (Washington, DC: The Catholic University of America Press, 2023).
2. Herbstrith, 65, my emphasis.
3. Herbstrith, 13.
4. Herbstrith, 172.
5. Edith Stein, *The Collected Works of Edith Stein, Volume Three, On the Problem of Empathy*, trans. Waltraut Stein, PhD (Washington, DC: ICS Publications, 1989).
6. Stein, 89, my emphasis.
7. Stein, 22–27.
8. Herbstrith, *Edith Stein*, 11.
9. Chiara Lubich, *Essential Writings*, 14.
10. Stein, *On the Problem of Empathy*, 89.
11. See Christopher Clark, *The Sleepwalkers: How Europe Went to War in 1914* (New York: HarperCollins, 2014).
12. Stein, *The Collected Works, Volume I, Life in a Jewish Family, Edith Stein: An Autobiography 1891–1916*, trans. Josephine Koeppel, OCD (Washington, DC: ICS Publications, 2016).
13. Stein, 331.
14. Stein, 338.
15. Stein, 360.
16. "Homily of John Paul II, For the Canonization of Edith Stein," Sunday, October 11, 1998. See https://www.vatican.va/content/john-paul-ii/en/

homilies/1998/documents/hf_jp-ii_hom_11101998_stein.html, accessed June 8, 2023.
17. See T.S. Eliot, *The Complete Poems and Plays* (London, UK: Faber & Faber, 2004), 189–190.
18. Edith Stein, *The Collected Works of Edith Stein, V: Self-Portrait in Letters 1916–1942*, trans. Josephine Koeppel, O.C.D. (Washington, DC: ICS Publications, 1993).
19. Stein, 37.
20. Herbstrith, *Edith Stein: A Biography*, 139.
21. Herbstrith, 139.
22. Stein, *Self-Portrait*, 54, my emphasis.

Eight: Viktor Frankl: A Why to Live For

1. See *The Solzhenitsyn Reader: Essential Writings 1947–2005*, eds. Edward E. Ericson, Jr. and Daniel J. Mahoney (Wilmington, DE: ISI Books, 2013), 253ff.
2. Viktor E. Frankl, *Man's Search for Meaning*, trans. Ilse Lasch (Boston, MA: Beacon Press, 2006).
3. Frankl, 76–77.
4. Frankl, 91.
5. Frankl, 89.
6. Frankl, 65.
7. Frankl, 65–66.
8. Frankl, 66, my emphasis.
9. Frankl, 79–80.
10. Frankl, 103.
11. Frankl, 111.
12. Frankl, 139.
13. Frankl, *139*.
14. *Papa Francesco: La Mia Idea di Arte*, ed. Tiziana Lupi (Milan: Mondadori, 2015), 14–15, my translation.
15. Frankl, 65–66.
16. Frankl, 111–112.
17. Augustine, *Confessions*, 10, XXVII. 38.
18. Frankl, *Man's Search for Meaning*, 111.
19. Frankl, 112.
20. Lubich, "Persons in Communion," in *Essential Writings*, 221–222.

Nine: Hannah Arendt: New Beginnings

1. Hannah Arendt, *Love and Saint Augustine* (Chicago, IL: The University of Chicago Press, 1996), 13.
2. (New York: Penguin Books, 2006). Hereafter, *Eichmann*. {there is Penguin New York too}
3. Arendt, *The Origins of Totalitarianism* (New York: Harcourt Brace, 1973).
4. Arendt, *The Human Condition* (Chicago, IL: The University of Chicago Press, 2018), 198.
5. Arendt, *The Last Interview and Other Conversations* (Brooklyn, NY: Melville House Publishing, 2013), 6.
6. Arendt, *The Human Condition*, 5, my emphasis.
7. Arendt, *Eichmann*, 48
8. Arendt, *The Life of the Mind* (New York: Harcourt Brace Jovanovich, 1978), 4-6.
9. Arendt, *Responsibility and Judgment*, ed. Jerome Kohn (New York: Schocken Books, 2003), 30, my emphasis.
10. Arendt, xv.
11. Arendt, *The Last Interview*, 43.
12. Arendt, *Eichmann*, 44.
13. Arendt, 48, my emphasis.
14. Arendt, 48.
15. Arendt, 49.
16. Arendt, 49–50.
17. Arendt, 48.
18. Arendt, 136.
19. Arendt, *Responsibility and Judgment*, 63.
20. Arendt, *Eichmann*, 137.
21. Arendt, *The Human Condition*, 9.
22. Arendt, 247.

Ten: Dietrich Bonhoeffer: Journey to the Center of the Person

1. Dietrich Bonhoeffer, *Letters and Papers from Prison*, trans. Isabel Best et al (Minneapolis, MN: Fortress Press, 2015). Hereafter, *Letters*. The classic biography is Eberhard Bethge, *Dietrich Bonhoeffer: A Biography* (Minneapolis, MN: Fortress Press, 2000).
2. Bonhoeffer, 369.

3. *The Collected Works of Eric Voegelin, Volume 31, Hitler and the Germans*, trans. Detlev Clemens and Brendan Purcell (Columbia, MI: University of Missouri Press, 1999), 17.
4. Alfred Delp. SJ, *Prison Writings* (Maryknoll, NY: Orbis Books, 2004), xxvii.
5. Delp, 91, my emphasis.
6. Dietrich Bonhoeffer, *Dietrich Bonhoeffer Works, Volume 3, Creation and Fall: A Theological Exposition of Genesis 1–3*, trans. Douglas Stephen Bax (Minneapolis, MN: Fortress Press, 2004). Hereafter, *Creation and Fall*.
7. See Susan Heschel, *The Aryan Jesus: Christian Theologians and the Bible in Nazi Germany* (Princeton, NJ: Princeton University press, USA, 2008).
8. Bonhoeffer, *Creation and Fall*, 64.
9. Bonhoeffer, 115.
10. Voegelin, *Hitler and the Germans*, 87.
11. Bonhoeffer, *Creation and Fall*, 115–120.
12. Bonhoeffer, 119–120, my emphasis.
13. Bonhoeffer, *Dietrich Bonhoeffer Works, Volume I, Sanctorum Communio: A Theological Study of the Sociology of the Church*, trans. Reinhard Kraus and Nancy Lukens (Minneapolis, MN: Fortress Press, 2009), 107.
14. Bonhoeffer, *Creation and Fall*, 145–146.
15. *Dietrich Bonhoeffer Works, Volume 6, Ethics*, trans. Reinhard Kraus et al (Minneapolis, MN: Fortress Press, 2009), 400.
16. Bonhoeffer, *Letters*, 485.
17. *Dietrich Bonhoeffer Works, Volume 4, Discipleship*, trans. Barbara Green and Reinhard Kraus (Minneapolis, MN: Fortress Press, 2003), 45.
18. Bonhoeffer, *Letters*, 217–219.
19. Bonhoeffer, 515.

Eleven: Alfred Delp SJ: Epiphany of the Person

1. Alfred Delp, SJ, *Prison Writings* (Maryknoll, NY: Orbis Books, 2004), xxi–xlii.
2. Delp, xxi–xii, my emphasis.
3. See *The Marx-Engels Reader*, ed. Robert C. Tucker (New York: W. W. Norton & Company, 1978), 473 ff. Hereafter, *Marx*.
4. *Marx*, 92.
5. See Mary Frances Coady, *With Bound Hands, A Jesuit in Nazi Germany: The Life and Selected Prison Letters of Alfred Delp* (Chicago, IL: Loyola Press, 2003), 97.
6. Pieper, "On the Christian Idea of Man," *The Review of Politics*, Volume 11, No. 1 (Jan. 1949), 3–16.

7. Coady, *With Bound Hands*, 96
8. Coady, 96–97, my emphasis.
9. Delp, *Prison Writings*, 89 ff.
10. Coady, *With Bound Hands*, 132,
11. See Robert Louis Stevenson, *Strange Case of Dr. Jekyll and Mr. Hyde*. Dr. Jekyll was outwardly good, but he also had an evil nature when he became a different person, that is, as in being Mr. Hyde. This aspect of the "doubleness" possible within human nature emerges in Gothic literature, for example, but also in the works of Fyodor Dostoevsky, as in his novella *The Double*. See *Notes from the Underground and the Double*, trans. Ronald Wilks (London: Penguin Classics, 2009).
12. Delp, *With Bound Hands*, 132.
13. Delp, *Prison Writings*, 22, my emphasis.
14. Delp, 23, my emphasis.
15. Delp, 35–36.
16. Delp, 53.
17. Delp, 53.
18. Delp, 80, my emphasis.
19. Delp, 82–83.
20. Chiara Lubich, 'The Divine Comedy,' unpublished.

Twelve: Emmanuel Levinas: A Spirituality of "Proximity"

1. John McNerney, "Emmanuel Levinas: Horizons on the Face of the 'Other.'" See https://voegelinview.com/emmanuel-levinas-horizons-on-the-face-of-the-other/, accessed June 23, 2023.
2. Emmanuel Levinas and Richard Kearney, "Dialogue with Emmanuel Levinas" in *Face to Face with Levinas*, ed. Richard Cohen (Albany, NY: State University of New York Press, 1986), 20.
3. David Walsh, *The Modern Philosophical Revolution*, 310.
4. Emmanuel Levinas, *Alterity and Transcendence*, trans. Michael B. Smith (New York: Columbia University Press, 1999), 27.
5. Levinas, 56.
6. Levinas, *Totality and Infinity: An Essay on Exteriority*, trans. Alfonso Lingis (Pittsburgh, PA: Duquesne University Press, 2007), 254.
7. Walsh, *The Modern Philosophical Revolution*, 310.
8. Levinas, *Alterity and Transcendence*, 88.
9. Levinas, 88, my emphasis.
10. Levinas, 98, my emphasis.

11. Levinas, 100.
12. Levinas, 99.
13. Levinas, 171.
14. *Unforeseen History*, trans. Nidra Poller (Chicago, IL: University of Illinois Press, 1994), 127.
15. Levinas, 128, my emphasis.
16. *On Escape, De l'évasion*, trans. Bettina Bergo (Stanford, CA: Stanford University Press, 2003), 97.
17. Levinas, *Unforeseen History*, 129.
18. Levinas, 129.
19. Levinas, *Collected Philosophical Papers*, trans. Alphonso Lingis (Pittsburgh, PA: Duquesne University Press, 1998), 167.
20. Levinas, 167.
21. Levinas, 43.

Thirteen: On the "Gravity" and "Grace" of *Who* We Are

1. See Simone Weil's "The *Iliad* or The Poem of Force," in *Simone Weil: An Anthology* (New York: Weidenfeld & Nicolson, 1986), 165. This essay was written during the first year of the Second World War and began as a reflection on the origins of Hitlerism.
2. Weil, 163, 165.
3. *Simone Weil: Late Philosophical Writings*, trans. Eric O. Springsted and Lawrence E. Schmidt (Notre Dame, IN: Notre Dame University Press, 2015), 135.
4. Weil, 134.
5. Karol Wojtyla, *Person and Act*, 617–618.
6. Simone Weil, *Gravity and Grace*, trans. Emma Crawford and Mario von der Ruhr (London: Routledge Classics, 2002), 179, my emphasis.
7. Weil, 180.
8. Weil, 180–181.
9. Weil, *An Anthology*, 71–72, my emphasis.
10. Weil, 203, my emphasis.
11. Weil, *Late Philosophical Writings*, 42.
12. Weil, 42.
13. Weil, 32.
14. Weil, 33.
15. Weil, 33.
16. Weil, *Waiting for God*, trans. Emma Craufurd (New York: Harper Perennial, 2009), 89.

17. *Gravity and Grace*, 12–15.
18. John Paul II, *On Human Work: Laborem Exercens*, 27. See https://www.vatican.va/content/john-paul-ii/en/encyclicals/documents/hf_jp-ii_enc_14091981_laborem-exercens.html.
19. John Paul II, *On Human Work*, 25.
20. Weil, *Gravity and Grace*, 181.
21. See Peter Salmon, *An Event, Perhaps: A Biography of Jacques Derrida*, 35.

Fourteen: Paul Ricoeur: Oneself as Another

1. Ricoeur, "Intellectual Autobiography," in *The Philosophy of Paul Ricoeur*, ed. Lewis Edwin Hahn (Chicago, IL: Open Court, 1996), 6. Hereafter, *The Philosophy of Paul Ricoeur*.
2. Ricoeur, 9.
3. Ricoeur, *Philosophy, Ethics and Politics*, tr, Kathleen Blamey (Cambridge, UK: Polity Press, 2020), 130.
4. There are references to Ricoeur in Karol Wojtyla's *Person and Act*. For example, he refers to Ricoeur in a discussion on "decision." See "decision is… a threshold through which the person as such goes out toward the good." See, for example, footnote 9, on page 230.
5. Ricoeur, *Philosophy, Ethics and Politics*, 129–130.
6. Ricoeur, 129, my emphasis.
7. Ricoeur, 18–19.
8. Ricoeur, *Oneself as Another*, trans. Kathleen Blamey (Chicago, IL: The University of Chicago Press, 1994).
9. See Ricoeur, "Sketch for a Plea for the Capable Human Being," in *Philosophy, Ethics and Politics*, 18.
10. Ricoeur, 19.
11. *Psychiatrie francaise* (June 1992), np.
12. Ricoeur, 119.
13. Ricoeur, 119.
14. Ricoeur, *Philosophical Anthropology: Writings and Lectures, Volume 3* (Cambridge, UK: Polity Press, 2016), 250–251.
15. *Philosophy, Ethics and Politics*, 119.
16. Ricoeur, 124, my emphasis.
17. Florence Gillet, *15 Days of Prayer with Blessed Chiara Badano* (Hyde Park, NY: New City Press, 2015), 101. See also *"In My Staying Is Your Going:" The Life and Thoughts of Chiara Luce Badano* (Hyde Park, NY: New City Press, 2021).
18. See *"In My Staying Is Your Going,"* 39.

Fifteen: Etty Hillesum: The Girl Who Learned to Kneel

1. Meins G.S. Coetsier *Etty Hillesum and the Flow of Presence: A Voegelinian Analysis* (Columbia, MO: University of Missouri Press, 2008), 6.
2. *Etty Hillesum: An Interrupted Life: The Diaries, 1941–1943 and Letters from Westerbork*, trans. Arnold J. Pomerans (New York: Henry Holt and Company, 1996), 143. Hereafter, *Diaries*.
3. Hillesum, *Diaries*, 153.
4. Hillesum, 38.
5. Hillesum, 39–40.
6. Hillesum, 140.
7. See *Reading Etty Hillesum in Context: Writings, Life, and Influences of a Visionary*, eds. Klaas Smelik, et al (Chicago, IL: University of Chicago Press, 2018).
8. Hillesum, *Diaries*, 88.
9. Henri Bergson, *Creative Evolution*, trans. Arthur Mitchell (New York: The Modern Library, 1944), 9.
10. Bergson, 10.
11. *The Solzhenitsyn Reader: New and Essential Writings 1947–2005*, eds. Edward E. Ericson, Jr. and Daniel J. Mahoney (Wilmington, DE: ISI Books, 2006), 267.
12. Hillesum, *Diaries*, 186.
13. Hillesum, 108.
14. Hillesum, 102–103.
15. Hillesum, 137.
16. Hillesum, 84.
17. Hillesum, 86.
18. *The Solzhenitsyn Reader*, 265, my emphasis.
19. Hillesum, *Diaries*, 207.
20. Hillesum, 211.
21. Hillesum, 212.
22. Hillesum, 122.
23. Hillesum, 245.
24. Hillesum, 245, 253.
25. Eric Voegelin calls this the "anthropological principle." The "anthropological principle" is Voegelin's term for Plato's comment that the polis is "man written large." See Brendan Purcell, "Introduction" in *Hitler and the Germans*, 25.

26. Hillesum, *Diaries*, 85.
27. Hillesum, 101.
28. Hillesum, 97.
29. Hillesum, 102. See Julian of Norwich, *Revelations of Divine Love*, trans. John Julian (Dulles, VA: Paraclete Press, 2011).
30. Hillesum, *Diaries*, 95.
31. Hillesum, 145.
32. Hillesum, 180–181.
33. Hillesum, 295.
34. Hillesum, 309.
35. Hillesum, 309, 228, my emphasis.
36. Hillesum, 105.
37. Hillesum, 332.
38. There are many studies on Etty Hillesum and the other women we have discussed. I refer readers, for example, to Rachel Feldhay Brenner, *Writing as Resistance: Four Women Confronting the Holocaust: Edith Stein, Simone Weil, Anne Frank, Etty Hillesum* (Pittsburgh, PA: Penn State University Press, 2003), and James Murphy, *Beauty and Horror in a Concentration Camp: The Story of Etty Hillesum* (Hyde Park, NY: New City Press, 2022).

Sixteen: Jacques Derrida: The Politics of Friendship

1. Peter Salmon, *An Event, Perhaps: A Biography of Jacques Derrida* (London: Verso, 2020), 253–254. A classic biography on Derrida is Benoît Peeters *Derrida: A Biography*, trans. Andrew Brown (Cambridge, UK: Polity Press, 2021).
2. David Walsh, *The Modern Philosophical Revolution*, 340–341.
3. Walsh, 340.
4. Derrida, *Margins of Philosophy*, trans. Alan Bass (Chicago, IL: The University of Chicago Press, 1982).
5. Derrida, *Limited Inc.*, trans. Gerald Graf et al. (Evanston, IL: Northwestern University Press, 1988), 8.
6. Derrida, *The Gift of Death and Literature in Secret*, trans. David Wills (Chicago, IL: The University of Chicago Press, 2008), 52.
7. Derrida, *The Politics of Friendship*, trans. George Collins (London: Verso, 2005).
8. Derrida, 230 ff.
9. Derrida, viii.
10. Derrida, 53.
11. Derrida, viii.

12. Derrida, 8-9. The term *"lovence"* is a neologism coined by Derrida.
13. Derrida, 7.
14. Derrida, 36.
15. Derrida, 306.
16. Lubich, *Essential Writings*, 247 ff.
17. Lubich, 254, my emphasis. See also Antonio M. Baggio, "Love of All Loves: Politics and Fraternity in the Charismatic Vision of Chiara Lubich," in *Claritas: Journal of Dialogue*, Volume 2, Number 2, October 2013.
18. Lubich, *Essential Writings*, 263.
19. Elena Merli, "The Church- a people of saints: The Prophetic insights of Iginio Giordani." See *Ekklesia Online*, https://www.ekklesiaonline.org/16-merli, July –September 2022, No. 16, accessed June 11, 2023. 3
20. Derrida, *The Politics of Friendship*, 306.

Seventeen: Pope Francis: The Forgotten Dimension of Fraternity

1. Pope Francis, *Fratelli Tutti: On Fraternity and Social Friendship*, October 2020. See https://www.vatican.va/content/francesco/en/encyclicals/documents/papa-francesco_20201003_enciclica-fratelli-tutti.html, accessed June 11, 2023. Throughout this chapter the encyclical citations are referred to by the numeric paragraphs in the original text.
2. Joseph Cardinal Ratzinger, *The Meaning of Christian Brotherhood* (San Francisco, CA: Ignatius Press, 1993).
3. See https://www.focolare.org/en/2020/10/05/maria-voce-an-appeal-for-fraternity/, accessed June 11, 2023.
4. Klaus Hemmerle, *Thesen zu einer trinitarischen Ontologie, English-Deutsche-Ausgabe* (Aachen: Echter, 2020), 114–115.
5. Pope Francis, *Let us Dream: The Path to a Better Future* (New York: Simon & Schuster, 2020), 4.

Eighteen: David Walsh: The Priority of the Person

1. David Walsh, *Guarded by Mystery: Meaning in a Postmodern Age* (Washington, DC: Catholic University of America Press, 1999), 26.
2. Levinas, *Of God Who Comes to Mind*, trans. Bettina Bergo (Stanford, CA: Stanford University Press, 1998), 15.
3. Oliver Goldsmith, 'The Deserted Village.' See https://www.poetryfoundation.org/poems/44292/the-deserted-village.
4. Goldsmith., 23–24.
5. Lubich, "The Attraction of Modern Times," in *Essential Writings*, 169.

6. McNerney, *Wealth of Persons: Economics with a Human Face.*
7. See David Walsh, "The Turn to the Subject as the Turn to the Person," paper prepared for a conference on "Subjectivity: Ancient and Modern," given on September 19-20, 2014, at Penn's View Hotel, Philadelphia, PA, Agora Institute, Eastern University. Later published in *The Priority of the Person.* See also Walsh's *The Modern Philosophical Revolution: The Luminosity of Existence* (Cambridge, MA: Cambridge University Press, 2008).
8. Walsh, "The Turn to the Subject as the Turn to the Person" in *The Priority of the Person*, 195-214.
9. Walsh, *The Modern Philosophical Revolution*, 76 ff, 80-90.
10. See Walsh's chapter on "Hegel's Inauguration of the Language of Existence" in *The Modern Philosophical Revolution*, 79.
11. Walsh, *The Priority of the Person*, 304, my emphasis.
12. Walsh, 305.
13. Walsh, *Guarded by Mystery*, 25-48.
14. See McNerney, *Wealth of Persons: Economics with a Human Face.*
15. Walsh, *Guarded By Mystery*, 26.
16. Walsh, *The Priority of the Person*, x.
17. (New York: HarperCollins, 1990), 34.
18. Walsh, *The Priority of the Person*, x.
19. See Fernando Pessoa, *The Book of Disquiet*, trans. Richard Zenith (London: Penguin Books, 2002), 104.
20. Walsh, *After Ideology: Recovering the Spiritual Foundations of Freedom* (New York: HarperCollins, 1990), 35.
21. (Columbia, OH: University of Missouri Press, 1997).
22. Walsh, *Growth of the Liberal Soul*, 246.
23. Walsh, *The Modern Philosophical Revolution*, xiii.
24. Walsh, 332.
25. Walsh, *The Politics of the Person*, 256.
26. Walsh, *The Priority of the Person*, x, my emphasis.
27. Walsh, 22.
28. Walsh, ix.
29. Walsh, 125.
30. Walsh, 6.
31. Interestingly, Hans Urs von Balthasar observes how the "turn to the person" can also be noted in the writings of Ludwig Feuerbach.
32. Walsh, *The Priority of the Person*, 3.
33. Walsh, 18.

34. "Cascando," *The Collected Poems of Samuel Beckett: A Critical Edition*, eds. Seán Lawlor and John Pilling (New York: Grove Press, 2012), 57.
35. Walsh, *The Priority of the Person*, 82.
36. Walsh, 7.
37. Walsh, 29.
38. Walsh, 31.
39. Walsh, 49.
40. See https://www.focolare.org/en/2016/01/10/un-patto-di-misericordia/, accessed June 12, 2023.
41. Walsh, *Growth of the Liberal Soul*, 51.
42. Walsh, *The Priority of the Person*, 104.
43. Walsh, 225.
44. Walsh, 233.
45. Walsh, 250, my emphasis.
46. Walsh, 263.
47. Walsh, 265.
48. Walsh, 266–268.
49. Aleksandr Solzhenitsyn, *November 1916: The Red Wheel, Knot II*, trans. H.T Willetts (New York: Farrar, Straus and Giroux, 2014), 1000.
50. Walsh, *The Priority of the Person*, 303 ff.

Afterword

1. Antonio Malo, "The Limits of Marion's and Derrida's Philosophy of the Gift," *International Philosophical Quarterly* 52, (2), 2012, 149–168. See also Jean-Luc Marion, *Being Given: Toward a Phenomenology of Givenness*, trans. Jeffrey L. Kosky (Stanford, CA: Stanford University Press, 2002).
2. Solzhenitsyn, *Invisible Allies* (New York: Counterpoint Press, 1997).
3. See Brendan Purcell, *Where is God in Suffering?* (Hyde Park, NY: New City Press, 2016). Purcell gives an in-depth consideration of Chiara Badano and others in this beautiful book.
4. Marion, *The Reason of the Gift*, trans. Stephen E. Lewis (Charlottesville, VA: University of Virginia Press, 2011), 63.
5. Solzhenitsyn, "Matryona's Home" in *The Solzhenitsyn Reader*, 24–56.
6. Solzhenitsyn, 56.

Selected Bibliography

Aristotle. *The Nicomachean Ethics*, trans. J.A.K. Thomson (Penguin Classics, 2004).

Arendt, Hannah. *Eichmann in Jerusalem: A Report on the Banality of Evil* (New York: Penguin Books, 2006).

Arendt. *The Human Condition* (Chicago, IL: The University of Chicago Press, 2018).

Arendt. *The Last Interview and Other Conversations* (Brooklyn, NY: Melville House Publishing, 2013).

Arendt. *The Origins of Totalitarianism* (New York: Harcourt Brace, 1979).

Baggio, Antonio, ed. *Il Principio Dimenticato: La Fraternità nella Politologica Contemporanea*, (Rome: Città Nuova, 2007).

Bethge, Eberhard. *Dietrich Bonhoeffer: A Biography* (Minneapolis, MN: Fortress Press, 2000).

Bonhoeffer, Dietrich. *Dietrich Bonhoeffer Works, vol. 1, Santorum Communio: A Theological Study of the Sociology of the Church*, trans. Reinhard Kraus and Nancy Lukens (Minneapolis, MN: Fortress Press, 2009).

Bonhoeffer. *Dietrich Bonhoeffer Works, vol. 3, Creation and Fall: A Theological Exposition of Genesis 1–3*, trans. Douglas Stephen Bax (Minneapolis, MN: Fortress Press, 2004).

Bonhoeffer. Dietrich Bonhoeffer Works, vol. 4, Discipleship, trans. Barbara Green and Reinhard Kraus (Minneapolis, MN: Fortress Press, 2003).

Bonhoeffer. *Dietrich Bonhoeffer Works, vol. 6, Ethics*, trans. Reinhard Kraus et al. (Minneapolis, MN: Fortress Press, 2008).

Bonhoeffer. *Dietrich Bonhoeffer Works, vol. 8, Letters and Papers from Prison*, trans. Isabel Best et al. (Minneapolis, MN: Fortress Press, 2015).

Buber, Martin. *I and Thou*, trans. Walter Kaufmann (New York: Simon & Schuster, 1996).

Coetsier, Meins G. S. *Etty Hillesum and the Flow of Presence: A Voegelinian Analysis, vol. 1* (Columbia, MO: University of Missouri Press, 2008).

Crosby, John F. *The Personalism of John Henry Newman* (Washington, DC: The Catholic University of America Press, 2016).

Derrida, Jacques. *Margins of Philosophy*, trans. Alan Bass (Chicago, IL: University of Chicago Press, 1982).

Derrida. *The Gift of Death and Literature in Secret*, trans. David Willis (Chicago, IL: The University of Chicago Press, 2008).

Derrida. *The Politics of Friendship*, trans. George Collins (London: Verso, 2020).

Douglass, Frederick. *Autobiographies, Narrative of the Life, My Bondage My Freedom, Life and Times* (New York: Library of America, 1994).

Douglass. *My Bondage and My Freedom* (London; Penguin Classics, 2003).

Douglass. *Narrative of the Life of Frederick Douglass, An African American Slave & Incidents in the Life of a Slave Girl, Harriet Jacobs* (New York: The Modern Library, 2000).

Fenton, Laurence. *Frederick Douglass in Ireland: The Black O'Connell* (Leicester, UK: Ulverscroft Press, 2014).

Francis. *Fratelli Tutti: The Encyclical Letter on Fraternity and Social Friendship*. Available online, see https://www.vatican.va/content/francesco/en/encyclicals/documents/papa-francesco_20201003_enciclica-fratelli-tutti.html

Francis. *Let us Dream: The Path to a Better Future* (New York: Simon & Schuster, 2020).

Frankl, Viktor. *Man's Search for Meaning*, trans. Ilse Lasch (Boston, MA: Beacon Press, 2006).

Geoghegan, Patrick M. *Liberator: The Life and Death of Daniel O'Connell 1830–1847* (Dublin: Gill & Macmillan, 2013).

Gillet, Florence. *15 Days of Prayer with Blessed Chiara Badano* (Hyde Park, NY: New City Press, 2015).

Herbstrith, Waltraud. *Edith Stein: The Untold Story of the Philosopher and Mystic Who Lost Her Life in the Death Camps of Auschwitz*, trans. Father Bernard Bonowitzz, O.C.S.O. (San Francisco, CA: Ignatius Press, 1992).

Hillesum, Etty. *An Interrupted Life: The Diaries, 1941–1945 and Letters from Westerbork*, trans. Arnold J. Pomerans (New York: Henry Holt and Company, 1996).

John Paul II. *Fides et Ratio: On the Relationship between Faith and Reason* (Boston, MA: Pauline Books and Media, 1998).

Kerr, Fergus. *"Work on Oneself:" Wittgenstein's Philosophical Psychology* (Washington, DC: The Catholic University of America Press, 2008).

Kierkegaard, Søren. *Either/Or, Part II*, eds. Howard V. Hong and Edna H. Hong (Princeton, NJ: Princeton University Press, 1990).

Kierkegaard. *Fear and Trembling: Dialectical Lyric by Johannes de Silentio* trans. Alasdair Hannay (London Penguin, 2003).

Kierkegaard. *The Journals of Kierkegaard*, trans. Alexander Dru (New York: Harper & Brothers, 1959).

Kierkegaard. *Stages on Life's Way*, trans. and eds. Howard V. Hong and Edna H. Hong (Princeton, NJ: Princeton University Press, 1991).

Kierkegaard. *Works of Love*, trans. and eds. Howard V. Hong and Edna H. Hong (Princeton, NJ: Princeton University Press, 1998).

Levinas, Emmanuel. *Alterity and Transcendence*, trans. Michael B. Smith (New York, Columbia Press, 1999).

Levinas. *Of God Comes to Mind*, trans. Bettina Bergo (Stanford, CA: Stanford University Press, 1998).

Levinas. *Totality and Infinity: An Essay on Exteriority*, trans. Alfonso Lingis (Pittsburg, PA: Duquesne Press, 2007).

Levinas. *Unforeseen History*, trans. Nida Poller (Chicago, IL: University of Illinois Press, 2004).

Lonergan, Bernard J. F. *Collected Works of Bernard Lonergan, vol. 3, Insight: A Study of Human Understanding*, eds. Frederick Crowe and Robert M. Doran (Toronto: University of Toronto Press, 2013).

Lubich, Chiara. *Essential Writings: Spirituality, Dialogue, Culture*, eds. Tom Masters and Callan Slipper (Hyde Park, NY: New City Press, 2007).

Lubich. *Paradise: Reflections on Chiara Lubich's Mystical Journey*, ed. Donald W. Mitchell (Hyde Park, NY: New City Press, 2020).

Macmurray, John. *Persons in Relation* (Atlantic Heights, NJ: Humanities Press, 1979).

MacNamara, Robert. *The Personalism of Edith Stein: A Synthesis of Thomism and Phenomenology* (Washington, DC: The Catholic University of America Press, 2023).

McNerney, John. *John Paul II: Poet and Philosopher* (London: T&T Clark, 2005).

McNerney. *Wealth of Persons: Economics with a Human Face* (Eugene, OR: Cascade Books, 2016).

Marcel, Gabriel. *Creative Fidelity*, trans. Robert Rosthal (New York: Fordham University Press, 2002).

Marcel. *Homo Viator: An Introduction to the Metaphysic of Hope*, trans. Emma Craufurd and Paul Seaton (South Bend, IN: St. Augustine's Press, 2010).

Marcel. *The Mystery of Being, vol. 1: Reflection and Mystery, Gifford Lectures 1949–1950*, trans. G.S. Fraser (South Bend, IN: St. Augustine's Press, 2001) and *Mystery of Being, vol. 2: Faith and Reality, Gifford Lectures 1949–1950*, trans. Rene Hague (South Bend, IN: St. Augustine's Press, 2001).

Monk, Ray. *Ludwig Wittgenstein: The Duty of Genius* (New York: Penguin Books, 1991).

Newman, John Henry. *An Essay in Aid of a Grammar of Ascent* (Notre Dame, IN: University of Notre Dame Press, 1992).

Newman. *The Idea of a University* (Notre Dame, IN: University of Notre Dame University Press, 2013).

Peeters, Benoît. *Derrida: A Biography*, trans. Andrew Brown (Cambridge, UK: Polity Press, 2013).

Purcell, Brendan. *From Big Bang to Big Mystery: Human Origins in the Light of Creation and Evolution* (Hyde Park, NY: New City Press, 2012).

Purcell. *Where is God in Suffering?* (Hyde Park, NY: New City Press, 2016).

Ratzinger, Joseph. *The Meaning of Christian Brotherhood* (San Francisco, CA: Ignatius Press, 1996).

Ricoeur, Paul. *Oneself as Another* (Chicago, IL: The University of Chicago Press, 1992).

Ricoeur. *Philosophical Anthropology: Writings and Lectures, vol. 3* (Cambridge, UK: Polity Press, 2016).

Ricoeur. *Philosophy, Ethics, and Politics*, trans. Kathleen Blamey (Cambridge, UK: Polity Press, 2020).

Ricoeur. *The Philosophy of Paul Ricoeur: An Anthology of His Work* (Boston, MA: Beacon Press, 1978).

Schlipp, Paul Arthur and Lewis Edwin Hahn, eds. *The Philosophy of Gabriel Marcel: The Library of Living Philosophers, vol. 12.* (La Salle, IL: Open Court, 1991).

Stein, Edith. *The Collected Works of Edith Stein, vol. 1, Life in a Jewish Family, Edith Stein: An Autobiography 1891–1916*, trans. Josephine Koeppel, OCD (Washington, DC: ICS Publications, 2016).

Stein. *The Collected Works of Edith Stein, vol. 3, On the Problem of Empathy*, trans. Waltraut Stein, PhD (Washington, DC: ICS Publications, 1989).

Stein. *The Collected Works of Edith Stein*, vol. 5: *Self-Portrait in Letters 1916–1942*, trans. Josephine Koppel, O.C.D. (Washington, DC: ICS, 1993).

Solzhenitsyn, Aleksandr. *November 1916: The Red Wheel, Knot II*, trans. H.T. Willetts (New York: Farrar, Straus and Giroux, 2014).

Solzhenitsyn. *The Solzhenitsyn Reader: New and Essential Writings 1947–2005*, eds. Edward E. Ericson, Jr. and Daniel J. Mahoney (Wilmington, DE: ISI Books, 2006).

Sweetman, Brendan, ed. *A Gabriel Marcel Reader*. (South Bend, IN: St. Augustine's Press, 2011).

Voegelin, Eric. *The Collected Works of Eric Voegelin*, vol. 31, *Hitler and the Germans*, trans. Detlev Clemens and Brendan Purcell (Columbia, MI: University of Missouri Press, 1999).

Walsh, David. *After Ideology: Recovering the Spiritual Foundations of Freedom* (New York: HarperCollins, 1990).

Walsh. *Guarded by Mystery: Meaning in a Postmodern Age* (Washington, DC: The Catholic University of America Press, 1999).

Walsh, *Politics of the Person as the Politics of Being* (Notre Dame, IN: University of Notre Dame University Press, 2016).

Walsh. *The Growth of the Liberal Soul* (Columbia, MI: University of Missouri Press, 1997).

Walsh. *The Modern Philosophical Revolution: The Luminosity of Existence* (New York: Cambridge University Press, 2008).

Walsh. *The Priority of the Person: Political, Philosophical, and Historical Discoveries* (Notre Dame, IN: Notre Dame University Press, 2020).

Weil, Simone. *Gravity and Grace*, trans. Emma Crawford and Mario von der Ruhr (London: Routledge Classics, 2002).

Weil. *Simone Weil: An Anthology* (New York: Weidenfeld & Nicolson, 1986).

Weil. *Simone Weil: Late Philosophical Writings*, trans. Eric O. Springsted and Lawrence E. Schmidt (Notre Dame, IN: Notre Dame University Press, 2015).

Weil. *Waiting for God*, trans. Emma Craufurd (New York: Harper Perennial, 2009).

Wittgenstein, Ludwig. *Culture and Value*, trans. Peter Winch (Chicago, IL: The University of Chicago Press, 1984).

Wittgenstein. *Philosophische Untersuchungen: Philosophical Investigations*, trans. G.E.M. Anscombe et al. (Oxford, UK: Blackwell Publishing, 2009).

Wittgenstein. *Tractatus Logico-Philosophicus*, trans. C.K. Ogden (Garden City, NY: Dover Publications, 1999).

Wojtyla, Karol. *Person and Act and Related Essays*, trans. Grzegorz Ignatik (Washington, DC: The Catholic University of America Press, 2021).

FOCOLARE MEDIA
Enkindling the Spirit of Unity

The New City Press book you are holding in your hands is one of the many resources produced by Focolare Media, which is a ministry of the Focolare Movement in North America. The Focolare is a worldwide community of people who feel called to bring about the realization of Jesus' prayer: "That all may be one" (see John 17:21).

Focolare Media wants to be your primary resource for connecting with people, ideas, and practices that build unity. Our mission is to provide content that empowers people to grow spiritually, improve relationships, engage in dialogue, and foster collaboration within the Church and throughout society.

 Visit www.focolaremedia.com to learn more about all of New City Press's books, our award-winning magazine *Living City*, videos, podcasts, events, and free resources.